American Wildflowers

American Wildflowers

Ann Reilly

PORTLAND HOUSE

NEW YORK

This 1991 edition published by Portland House,
a division of dilithium Press, Ltd.
distributed by Outlet Book Company, Inc.,
a Random House Company,
225 Park Avenue South, New York, New York 10003

ISBN 0-517-05072-0
8 7 6 5 4 3 2 1

Printed and bound in Italy

For rights information about the photographs in
this book please contact:

The Image Bank
111 Fifth Avenue, New York, NY 10003

Writer: Ann Reilly

Producer: Solomon M. Skolnick
Designer: Ann-Louise Lipman
Editor: Sara Colacurto
Production: Valerie Zars
Senior Picture Researcher: Edward Douglas
Editorial Assistant: Carol Raguso
Project Picture Researcher: Robert V. Hale

i *Rudbeckia fulgida,* coneflower.
ii *Eschscholtzia californica,* California poppy.

Table of Contents

Daisy Family

Snapdragon Family

Lily Family

Buttercup Family

Carrot Family

Pea Family

Bluebell Family

Violet Family

Milkweed Family

Purslane Family

Evening Primrose Family

Gentian Family

Mint Family

Poppy Family

Primrose Family

Geranium Family

Phlox Family

Iris Family

Madder Family

Flax Family

Water Lily Family

Introduction

A wildflower is any plant that will grow, bloom, and reproduce without human intervention. Wildflowers need only the help of nature to add their beauty to the landscape. No matter how hostile the environment, these plants will find a home: on frigid mountaintops, on baking-hot deserts, in humid jungles, on sweeping prairies, or in salty marshes. Wildflowers thrive along roadsides, in empty fields, under the shaded canopy of trees, and on the sides of ponds and streams.

Wildflowers are often called native plants, a term that is not totally correct. While all wildflowers were at one time native to a particular area, civilization has, either purposely or accidentally, caused them to grow far beyond their original homes. The earliest explorers to the Orient, for instance, brought Asian wildflowers back to Europe, and early American settlers introduced European wildflowers into America. As new lands continued to be explored and new plants were discovered, many wildflowers were distributed worldwide.

Our ancestors used wildflowers for a number of medicinal, as well as culinary, purposes, some of which are still valid; others have proved to be no more than old wives' tales. No matter, for wildflowers can be enjoyed simply for their beauty and for the study of the interdependency among the various members of the natural world.

In the orderly world of scientists, and, in particular, the scientific world of taxonomy—the classification of living things according to family, genus, and species—there is a place for everything and everything is in its place. But "where the wild things grow," their names grow wild as well—and a rose by any other name may, indeed, not be a rose at all.

For example, many plants known as lilies are not in the lily genus, *Lilium,* at all. They are known as lilies only because the flowers look like lilies, with six pointed flaring petals. There are at least three plants known commonly as coneflowers that are in three different genera: black-eyed Susan is sometimes called coneflower, and there are purple coneflowers and prairie coneflowers. The common name stems from the fact that the central portion of the flower is cone-shaped.

There are four plants known as cowslip in different parts of the country—the shooting star, marsh marigold, Virginia bluebell, and one of the primroses—that are in four separate genera and three different plant families. Although there is some doubt as to how plants became known as cowslips, it is thought that the name derived from cow slop. Since these plants grow abundantly where cows graze, the superstition arose that they sprang from cow manure.

To make plant identification even more confusing, some plants are known by more than one common name, often because of local custom. It is therefore essential when speaking of plants to always include their Latin, or botanical, names, as these do not vary.

The pages that follow will introduce 21 families of glorious wildflowers, first in words, then in pictures. The history, myths, and legends associated with them are explored in the text, while the photos reveal their superb beauty. From the earliest days of spring to the final days of fall, these wildflowers contribute diverse colors, forms, and sizes to a vast and fascinating world.

DAISY FAMILY

There are literally thousands of daisies, or plants with daisylike flowers, in the *Compositae*, or Daisy Family, the largest plant family on earth. The Latin name *Compositae* refers to the fact that all flowers in this family are made up of two kinds of flowers: the ray flowers (petals) and the disk flowers in the center. Estimates by botanists put the number of plants in this family at about 20,000. The Daisy Family comprises chrysanthemums, fleabanes, coreopsis, black-eyed Susans and other coneflowers, sunflowers, blanket-flowers, dandelions, chicory, Joe Pye weed, asters, goldenrod, and blazing stars.

The name *daisy* is a shortened version of Chaucer's "dayeseye," which refers to those flowers that open only during the day. The English daisy, *Bellis perennis*, is a true "dayeseye," a low-growing biennial with single or double flowers and white, pink, or red petals surrounding yellow centers. This plant is now cultivated in formal gardens, but it can also be seen growing in the wild and, occasionally, on lawns. When it grows among tall grass, the basal, spoon-shaped leaves grow upright, but when on lawns, the leaves lie flat on the ground.

Many (but certainly not all) members of the Daisy Family are in the *Chrysanthemum* genus. The most common daisy in the wildflower world is the ox-eye daisy, *Chrysanthemum leucanthemum*, with white petals and bright yellow centers blooming on plants as tall as two and one-half feet. Once native to Europe and Asia, the ox-eye now grows wild throughout North America. The British called this plant thunderflower, since it blooms during the summer, when thunderstorms are common; they also believed it had the power to keep lightning from striking, so it was often hung in doorways.

Bruisewort is another common English name for the ox-eye, because the crushed leaves were used to soothe bruised skin, while the dried stems and blossoms were boiled and made into a concoction to heal chapped skin. Ox-eye extract was used to treat smallpox, tumors, jaundice, broken bones, and toothaches. It was believed that to dream of a daisy in the fall meant a winter of bad fortune was ahead, but to dream of daisies in the spring augured good luck.

Like most of its relatives, the ox-eye daisy makes an excellent cut flower. Many of the wild chrysanthemums were hybridized to develop the florists' chrysanthemum, *C. X morifolium*, one of the most popular plants in the cut-flower industry and a fall garden favorite.

The arctic daisy hails from the far north. Native to coastal Alaska, *C. arcticum* has lobed leaves and white flowers with yellow centers. The tricolor chrysanthemum, *C. carinatum*, has a purple center; it has white, yellow, red, or purple petals and a band of a different color at the base of the petals, hence the flower's name. It is a native of Morocco.

The garland chrysanthemum, or crown daisy, *C. coronarium*, is originally from the Mediterranean, but today it is widely grown in the Orient, where its leaves are eaten as greens and its flower heads are used as garnish. It has a thick, branched stem and yellow to white flowers.

The marguerite, or Paris daisy, *C. frutescens*, is a bushy plant with white or yellow petals. It is originally from the Canary Islands but became popular in France, which is how it obtained its second common name. It is often grown as a garden plant and makes a good cut flower.

The Shasta daisy, *C. X superbum*, is a hybrid of *C. maximum*, the max chrysanthemum. The max chrysanthemum is a wildflower from the Pyrenees with large white petals. Feverfew, *C. parthenium*, by contrast, has large clusters of very small flowers that sometimes have no petals.

The natural insecticide pyrethrum is made from *C. cinerariifolium*, the Dalmatian insect flower, or, more simply, pyrethrum. Native to Yugoslavia, it has white petals with yellow centers and is grown in various places around the world, including Japan and East Africa, where the insecticide is extracted from the dried flower heads. *C. coccineum* is also called pyrethrum, as well as painted daisy and Persian insect flower; it too is a source of the insecticide. *C. coccineum's* petals are white, pink, or red, surrounding yellow centers.

The herb costmary, *C. balsamita*, sometimes known as mint geranium or alecost, is another member of the *Chrysanthemum* genus. This plant was used to flavor ale and beer before brewers used hops. Costmary was also known in early America as Bibleleaf, because churchgoers used it as a bookmark and nibbled on the leaves to keep awake during sermons. The leaves are oblong and curled, slightly fragrant, and have a slight balsam flavor. The plant rarely blooms, but when it does, its petals are white. Costmary is used fresh or dried and can be added to soups, stews, and salads.

Another popular "composite" wildflower is *Erigeron*, commonly known as fleabane. The suffix *bane* comes from an old English word meaning "destroyer." It was believed that these plants would rid homes and other places of fleas; the plant juice was applied to the body and dried stalks and leaves were burned to fumigate buildings. Fleabane was also dried and stuffed into mattresses, but it is no longer believed to have insect-repelling value.

The genus name *Erigeron* comes from two Greek words meaning "spring" and "old man"; the flowers are thought by imaginative people to look like an old man's beard, and the plants start to bloom in the spring. An old English name for this plant is robin's plantain, given because the seeds were believed to have been imported to Europe inside a stuffed bird. An old superstition says that if an expectant woman wants to know the sex of her child, she should plant the seeds of fleabane: if the flowers are pink, the baby will be a girl; if they are blue, it will be a boy.

Daisy fleabane, *E. philadelphicus*, has small flowers with white to pink petals that bloom in loose clusters above oblong leaves. It is as soft and as delicate as baby's breath. Yellow fleabane, *E. linearis*, has yellow blooms. Its Latin name is descriptive of the narrow, grasslike, linear leaves found at the base of the plant.

Sneezeweed is the common name given to another group of plants with composite flowers, the *Heleniums*, named for Helen of Troy. Native Americans used the powdered flower heads of sneezeweed as snuff to induce violent sneezing and rid the body of evil spirits; the pollen, however, is very heavy and cannot be carried by the wind, and thus it does not generally cause allergies. Several species are known to be toxic to sheep.

The most common wildflower in the genus is *H. autumnale*, which blooms in the fall and has yellow to orange flowers on two- to four-foot plants. Bitterweed, *H. amarum*, like others in the genus, has golden-yellow flowers. The center of the flower is dome-shaped and its petals have ragged edges; the plants are bushy and clothed in narrow leaves. Cows that eat bitterweed produce bitter milk.

The tidy tips genus, *Layia*, was named for George Tradescant Lay, a botanist who participated in plant expeditions to California in the early 1800's.

Tidy tips is a name shared by many of the 15 members of the genus, because the notched, yellow petals are neatly tipped with white. A common sight in early summer, California fields is *L. platyglossa*, which grows to about one foot and has two-inch flowers, typical of tidy tips. The species name *platyglossa* means "flat-tongued" and refers to the shape of the petals. *L. chrysanthemoides* has notched petals surrounding a brown-speckled center and is common in the California coastal mountains. A few species of tidy tips have solid yellow flowers, and the white daisy, *L. glandulosa*, has pure white flowers.

After tidy tips bloom, they produce fine, tufted seeds that resemble those of the dandelion and are easily carried in the summer breezes. When dropped, the seeds may lie dormant until the following year's spring rains cause them to germinate.

Coreopsis, or tickseed, is so named because the seeds are flat and narrow and have two winglike projections extending from their sides, like a tick. Coreopsis has daisylike flowers, but it can be distinguished from many other members of the Daisy Family by the jagged notches that appear in the petal tips.

The genus name *Coreopsis* is derived from two Greek words: *koris*, which means "bedbug," and *opsis*, which means "resembling"; apparently some people felt that the seeds looked like a bedbug rather than a tick. Early American settlers placed the seeds in their mattresses, because they believed that they repelled fleas and bedbugs, as well as other insects.

There are both annual and perennial members of the *Coreopsis* genus. *C. lanceolata* is a perennial with basal, lance-shaped leaves and flowers with eight petals. *C. verticillata*, also a perennial, has narrow, needlelike leaves, as do all plants whose names include the word *verticillata*; its yellow flowers cover the mounded plants. *C. tinctoria*, sometimes called *calliopsis*, is an annual with airy leaves resembling those of a fern. The flowers may be yellow, red, or yellow with a ring of red around the center.

Another member of the Daisy Family, the black-eyed Susan—either the perennial *Rudbeckia fulgida* or the annual *R. hirta*—is a native of the midwestern United States, but it was accidentally introduced into the east years ago in a bag of clover seed. It fills fields and roadsides with bright, golden, daisylike flowers throughout the summer and has become so entrenched in the east that Maryland has designated it as its state flower.

Pollinated by insects and wind, the black-eyed Susan was named in honor of Olaf Rudbeck, a Swedish botanist, who is considered the father of modern botany and who was a teacher of Caroleus Linnaeus, the eighteenth-century botanist responsible for devising taxonomy. The "black eye" is really the central disk of the flower and is actually more dark brown than black; no one is quite sure who Susan was.

The black-eyed Susan flourishes in poor soil and over-grazed pastures, taking over when the desired plants or crops have been eliminated. The two- to three-foot stems and the leaves of black-eyed Susans are covered with coarse hair, which helps them withstand drought conditions by trapping and retaining moisture. The hair also makes this plant unpalatable to wild animals, livestock, and crawling insects.

Sometimes called golden glow, *R. laciniata* blooms in midsummer. Its flowers are smaller than those of other black-eyed Susans, but there are more of them. It blooms in the shade or woodland borders, as well as in full sun, if it has enough water. The clasping coneflower, *Dracopis amplexi-caulis* (once called *R. amplexicaulis*) is an annual named for the shape of its leaves.

A solution made from black-eyed Susans was once used to treat skin disorders, and modern science has determined that the plant does, in fact, contain natural antibodies. A tough and reliable plant, it has been hybridized by modern plant breeders to create such garden plants as the gloriosa daisy.

Although many rudbeckias are known as coneflowers, because the central disk of the flower is often cone-shaped, this common name is shared by other wildflowers, particularly those in the *Echinacea* genus—the purple coneflowers. The most common is *E. purpurea*, which has drooping purple petals surrounding a central cone ringed with spiny bristles.

The Latin name, *Echinacea*, is a derivative of the Greek word *echinos*; it means "hedgehog" or "sea urchin," referring to the bristles on the central part of the flower. This hardy perennial has thick, black edible roots that were once eaten to increase the body's resistance to infection. Tinctures of the root were used in folk medicine as a remedy for corns.

Another genus of coneflowers is the prairie coneflower, *Ratabida*. It is often called Mexican hat because of the height of the cone—one to two inches—and because it is surrounded by drooping petals, making the flower look like a sombrero. When the dark purple, tubular flowers start to bloom at the bottom of the cone, they look like a hatband.

The Mexican hat's cone has an aniselike odor when crushed. Native Americans extracted an orange-yellow dye from the flowers and brewed tea from both its flowers and leaves.

The most common species of prairie coneflower is *R. columnifera*. One variety of this species has only yellow flowers and another has red petals touched with yellow at the tips, giving it the name red Mexican hat.

Another midwestern native in the Daisy Family is the common sunflower, *Helianthus annuus*, which is the state flower of Kansas and the floral emblem for the Soviet Union. The common sunflower can grow to 10 feet in height and has flowers that are three to six inches across; the giant sunflower, *H. giganteus*, can reach heights of 12 feet and has even larger flowers. Both are native to the dry plains; they are drought tolerant and love the heat and brightness of the sun.

The genus name for the sunflower comes from two Greek words: *helios*, which means "sun," and *anthos*, which means "flower." The large, daisylike flowers are easy to recognize, as are the giant seed heads that are the source of a favorite snack treat—sunflower seeds—for children and adults alike.

Although sunflowers are native to the United States and Mexico, they were also known to the Incas in Peru, who revered them as representatives of a sun god. The Incas made necklaces of these golden flowers that were worn by the priestesses in the temple of the sun. The early Spanish explorers, particularly Pizarro, took sunflowers back to Spain with them. Centuries later, they were reintroduced to their home, the United States, as cultivated plants.

Northern tribes of Native Americans grew sunflowers along the shores of the Great Lakes and used the ground-up seeds for flour and the oil extracted from the flower for cooking, mixing paints, and conditioning their hair. The nineteenth-century American settlers planted sunflowers near their homes, as they believed the plants would protect them from malaria. They used the leaves and stalks for cattle fodder and fibers from the stems for cloth. Dried leaves were smoked like tobacco, and the seeds were used to make coffee. The settlers also made soap from the oil and a color-fast yellow dye from the petals.

The narrow-leaved or swamp sunflower, *H. angustifolius*, is found east of the Mississippi River in moist, boggy areas, although it, too, is drought tolerant. *H. grosseserratus*, the sawtooth or big-toothed sunflower, blooms in the fall and has flowers over deeply toothed leaves.

Closely related to the sunflower is the giant Jerusalem artichoke, *H. tuberosus*. It is neither an artichoke nor from Jerusalem (it is native to the eastern United States and Canada); the name Jerusalem is a corruption of the Italian word *girasole*, which means "turning to the sun," as the flower heads follow the sun throughout the day. This happens because light inhibits their stem growth, and so the shaded side grows faster than the side facing the sun, tipping the flowers over toward the light.

The tuberous root of the Jerusalem artichoke has been eaten for centuries—raw, boiled, or baked; Lewis and Clark were fed Jerusalem artichoke in 1805 by a native squaw in the North Dakota region.

A dwarf version of the stately sunflower is the mountain sunflower, *Hymenoxys acaulis*. It grows only one foot tall and has notched yellow petals and a domed center. Western cattlemen watch for these plants on their ranges, because they are a sign of overgrazing. Sheep farmers dread their appearance as well, because at least two species of mountain sunflower are poisonous to sheep.

The mountain sunflower is also commonly called old man of the mountain, alpine sunflower, and sun god, because it can be found growing high on mountaintops above the timber line and the flowers face east, toward the rising sun.

*M*embers of the *Gaillardia* genus are called blanketflower or Indian blanket, because the flowers have the same red, orange, and golden tones as the blankets woven by the Native Americans of the southwestern United States, where the plants originate. The genus was named for Gaillard de Marentoneua, a French botanist. It was introduced into Europe in the early 1800's and has long been prized for its long blooming period and drought resistance.

The *Gaillardia* genus contains the annual *G. pulchella* and the perennial *G. aristata*. The perennial blanketflower has flowers with yellow- and red-toothed petals and red-domed centers. The annual blanketflower is very similar in appearance to the perennial, but the flowers are smaller. Both are long-lasting garden flowers; they bloom all summer and make excellent cut flowers as well. The arrangement of the colorful petals on the daisylike flower has given it a third common name, fire wheel.

*T*he dandelion derived its name from the French *dent de lion*, which means "lion's tooth," describing the toothed margins of the leaves. If the plant grows in full sun, the teeth will be much deeper than if it grows in the shade. The bright yellow heads of the flowers will form, however, only if the plant grows in full sun.

The genus name for dandelion, *Taraxacum*, comes from an Arabic word meaning "bitter herb." This plant is sometimes called tramp with the golden head, as it can quickly "tramp" through barren fields and cultivated lawns. Its leaves exude ethylene gas, which prevents other plants from growing close to it. Many consider the common dandelion, *Taraxacum officinale*, to be a vicious weed, but others appreciate its food value, particularly in salads, and purposely include it in gardens. It was actually brought to North America to be used as a garden plant but soon escaped into the wild. Now it is found everywhere in the world, except in the tropics and the desert.

Once the yellow flowers have faded, the characteristic, rounded, and fluffy seed heads form, spreading like parachutes in the wind to quickly grow into new plants. Children have always helped the dandelion to spread, perhaps unwittingly, by blowing the seeds from the stems to watch them float away. Some believe that if the seeds are blown off all in one breath, a secret wish will come true. Another superstition says that blowing the seeds toward a loved one will send secret words of love along to that person.

Once blown from the stem, the soft seeds can remain in the air almost indefinitely, provided the humidity is below 70 percent. When the humidity rises, the seeds will drop to earth and germinate with the help of rain.

Dandelions contain high amounts of vitamins A and C and have been used since ancient times in folk medicines. Drinking a cup of dandelion tea every morning and every evening was believed to prevent rheumatism. The Dutch believed that eating dandelion salad on Monday and Thursday was necessary to stay healthy. In the eighteenth century, King Frederick of Prussia was cured of dropsy (edema) with dandelions; in the nineteenth, dandelions were used to cure impetigo and liver ailments. Over the years dandelions have also been used to treat congestion, fever, and even hypochondria.

The fall dandelion, *Leontodon autumnalis,* is similar in appearance to the *Taraxacum* dandelion, but it blooms in late summer and fall instead of spring and has a more wiry stem. This plant's generic name also means "lion's tooth," which describes the shape of its leaves.

Mountain dandelions of the genus *Agoseris* are sometimes known as false dandelions. Their flower stems are not hollow like those of the true dandelions, and their milky sap contains more latex and can be chewed once it is dried. The young leaves are tasty and have been used in salads, and its flowers are used to make tea, wine, and beer.

Chicory, *Cichorium intybus,* is almost as common a wildflower as the dandelion, and it shares many of the same culinary uses. It is a ragged-looking plant, with deeply toothed basal leaves and bright blue shaggy flowers whose petal edges are notched, or jagged, like daisies. There is a legend that Florilor, a kind lady who rejected the advances of the sun god, was changed into chicory. Ignoring his presence, she closed her flowers at noon. And true to the legend, chicory flowers stay open only until noon, when they close up and avoid the sun completely. On rainy days, the flowers do not open at all. The bright blue of chicory seems to reflect the color of the sky and is particularly brilliant against the glare of sandy beaches.

While chicory is often associated with the New Orleans French Quarter and chicory coffee, knowledge of the plant actually dates back to the ancient Egyptians, Romans, and Greeks, who drank a chicory brew because they believed it was good for the liver and the gall bladder. In Europe, chicory was grown for cattle fodder as well as for salad greens. It has also been used as a love potion, to prevent scurvy, as a mild sedative, and for skin irritations. Chicory is related to endive and escarole and can be grown indoors as a delicately flavored salad green known as French endive or Belgian endive.

Desert chicory, *Rafinesquia neomaxicana,* is native to dry areas and blooms in the late winter and early spring, with flowers that have notched white petals veined in pinkish purple.

Clearly, Native Americans have had a strong influence on the development of names and uses for wildflowers. There is a popular belief that Joe Pye weed, *Eupatorium purpureum,* was named for a medicine man named Joe Pye who taught early settlers how to use the plant to relieve typhoid fever. Perhaps a more likely theory is that the name comes from the Native American word for typhoid, *jopi,* which then became anglicized to Joe Pye.

In the southern Appalachian mountains, Joe Pye weed is called queen-of-the-meadow, a good name for this stately plant with clusters of slightly fragrant, pinkish purple flowers that bloom in moist summer meadows. Other names for the plant are Indian sage, kidney root, gravel root, and sweet Joe Pye weed. The genus name comes from Mithridates Eupator, a Persian general who successfully defeated the Romans on several occasions and who used the plant as something of a magic potion in the belief that this would ensure victory.

Native Americans used Joe Pye weed in a number of ways. It was used to increase the appetite and soothe the nerves, and, if used on a regular basis, the crushed leaves, which have an odor similar to vanilla, were believed to improve the complexion. A hot tea made from the leaves was used to break a fever, and the Iroquois used the plant to treat kidney disorders. Braves also believed it improved their chances of winning over women whom they courted.

Relatives of Joe Pye weed were used as aperitifs and to treat dropsy, liver diseases, skin diseases, ulcers, and scabies. The Creoles used them in antidotes for snake bites and other poisons. Several related species of Joe Pye weed include spotted Joe Pye weed, *E. maculatum*, which has purple or purple-spotted stems, a defense mechanism for the plant against sunburn; hollow Joe Pye weed, *E. fistulosum*, which has hollow 10-foot stems; and *E. dubium*, a smaller plant with egg-shaped leaves. Hardy ageratum, or mistflower, *E. coelestinum*, is so known because its blue flowers resemble the garden annual, *Ageratum houstonianum*, which has the same common names.

Western Joe Pye weed, *E. occidentale*, is similar to its eastern cousin, sweet Joe Pye weed, but is a smaller-growing plant. Two relatives with white flowers are thoroughwort, *E. perfoliatum*, which grows in moist woods and marshes, and white snakeroot, *E. rugosum*, a toxic plant. Thoroughwort was once called boneset and was applied to broken bones in the belief that it would speed healing, a folk remedy that has never been proven.

*T*he Greeks believed that the aster grew when Virgo, looking down from heaven, started to cry and scattered stardust on the earth. In fact, the genus name, *Aster*, is derived from *aster*, the Greek word for "star."

The ancient Greeks used asters on altars to keep evil spirits away, and wreaths of aster flowers were placed in temples for celebrations. The Greeks also thought that the plant kept snakes away and applied it to snakebites to stop the spread of venom. At one time, asters were believed to cure the bite of a rabid dog. They were also regarded as a symbol of elegance and love.

The medieval French superstitiously called the aster eye of Christ, and the Germans and English called it starwort, burning it to keep evil spirits away. In America, the Shakers used asters in cosmetics to keep the skin clear; people also placed aster leaves near beehives in the belief that they would improve the honey.

Several asters are known as Michaelmas daisies, because they bloom in late September at the same time as the Feast Day of St. Michael the Archangel. Although few asters bloom in December, the name Christmas daisy has been given to some.

There are perhaps as many as 500 to 600 species of aster, and many are so similar in appearance that it is difficult to differentiate among them. All, however, provide large splashes of primarily violet, purple, or blue daisylike flowers in open fields or at woods edge in late summer and fall.

One of the most common asters is the New England aster, *A. novaeangliae*. It has pinkish lilac to purple shaggy flowers, depending on the location and the soil; it grows best where its roots are cool and moist. The flowers defy the first frost, blooming well into late fall, and make long-lasting cut flowers. The New England aster is the parent of many garden varieties of aster.

The stiff aster, *A. linariifolius*, is a smaller plant, about two feet tall, with flowers that are more blue-toned than the New England aster's. The stiff aster can be recognized by its wiry stems and needlelike leaves, and it is sometimes called sandpaper aster or pine starwort. In contrast with this is *A. foliaceus*, the leafy aster, which has purple flowers and large lance-shaped leaves. The blue wood aster, *A. cordifolius*, has yet another type of leaf—heart-shaped—and clusters of tiny blue or violet flowers on six-foot stems.

The smooth aster, *A. laevis*, is one of the few asters whose seeds do not need to go through stratification—a period of cold—to germinate. The smooth aster will therefore reproduce and bloom more quickly than the others.

Most asters grow in dry conditions, but the sea aster, *A. tripolium*, favors salt marshes and tidal estuaries. The bluish purple petals are set off by a fragrant central disk of yellow.

*E*nglish gardens are often filled with goldenrods. Brought to Europe from America, they are still regarded by many as weeds, although some species are beautiful wildflowers truly deserving of cultivation. Goldenrods are the state flowers of Kentucky and Nebraska.

The goldenrod has long been considered a symbol of good fortune and treasure. One old superstition says that if a piece of goldenrod is carried in one's pocket, it will bring good luck.

The botanical name for goldenrod, *Solidago*, comes from the Latin *solidare*, meaning "to strengthen," because the plant was once believed to have medicinal powers. During the reign of Queen Elizabeth I, goldenrod powder was sold in England for its healing qualities. Native Americans used goldenrod in a unique steam bath: It was mixed with water and other wildflowers and herbs and boiled; the hot pot was then set on the ground with a sick patient and both were covered with a tent of blankets. Only after the ailing patients had sweated out their "evil spirits" (disease) did they emerge from their tents. The colonists used goldenrod in tea, especially after the Boston Tea Party, when tea was in short supply, but this is no longer recommended because of a poisonous fungus that often grows on the plants.

Goldenrods contain a small amount of rubber, which can be increased by plant-breeding methods. This has been the subject of scientific research to see whether it is economically feasible to grow goldenrod for its rubber content.

Because goldenrods are the most obvious weeds in bloom in the fall at the height of the hay-fever season, they have long been unjustly blamed for causing people to sneeze. Actually, the true culprits are ragweeds (*Ambrosia* species), as goldenrod pollen is too heavy to blow in the wind.

There are about 130 different species of goldenrod, but many of these cross-pollinate so freely that it is hard to distinguish among them. The common names of many of the most recognized plants describe their characteristics. For example, there is rough-leaved goldenrod, *S. rugosa*; blue-stemmed goldenrod, *S. caesia*; plume, or early goldenrod, *S. juncea*; tall goldenrod, *S. altissima*; and grass-leaved goldenrod, *S. graminifolia*.

The seaside goldenrod, *S. sempervirens*, fills the dunes with gold along the coasts of Cape Cod and Long Island. The plant attracts the monarch butterfly as the insect migrates. The seaside goldenrod does not need wet soil but is tolerant of salt spray and brackish water. The sweet goldenrod, *S. odora*, has a pleasing aniselike scent when the leaves are crushed. Such species as European goldenrod, *S. Virgaurea*; California goldenrod, *S. californica*; and Canada or meadow goldenrod, *S. canadensis*, are found where their names suggest.

The alpine goldenrod, *S. multiradiata*, is one of the lowest-growing goldenrod plants, reaching a height of only 18 inches. The silverrod, or white goldenrod, *S. bicolor*, has bicolored yellow and white flowers. The gray goldenrod, *S. nemoralis*, has hairy gray-green stems and leaves covered with gray hairs.

*L*ate-season color is always provided by the blazing star in the *Liatrus* genus, a genus of about 40 species that hybridize freely, making their identification somewhat difficult.

Adding to the confusion is the number of other wildflowers that share the same common name as the blazing star but are in no way related.

When the first pioneers crossed the prairies of the midwest, they found the blazing star growing side by side with goldenrod. The flowers are bright pinkish purple and jagged, giving rise to another descriptive name, gayfeather. Unlike the blooming of most flowering plants, its blooming starts at the top of the spike and works downward.

Gayfeathers are members of the Daisy Family, but only close examination can confirm this, because the flowers are actually central disks with no petals and because so few members of the Daisy Family bloom in spikes. The plant's stiff, erect stems are covered with rough, grayish hairs and long, thin leaves.

The spiked gayfeather, *L. spicata*, is the most common wildflower in the *Liatrus* genus. As the seeds of this plant form, a long, feathery bristle called a *pappus* develops from what was the base of the flower. The rough blazing star, *L. aspera*, is lower-growing, and its flowers are segmented along the stem instead of being in a continuous spike. The spiked gayfeather is found in marshes and wet prairies, whereas the rough blazing star thrives in drier conditions.

The prairie blazing star, *L. pycnostachya*, has lavender flowers that occur densely along a wandlike stem covered with hairy, grasslike leaves. It is also called tall blazing star, thick-spike gayfeather, or button snakeroot, for the clusters of flowers that look like buttons and for the way the fibrous roots "snake" from the corm. The dotted gayfeather, *L. punctata*, is also called button snakeroot. It received the former common name from the spots that appear on its leaves.

*A*lthough yarrows don't look like daisies, they are in the Daisy Family.

The yarrow, a wildflower in the *Achillea* genus, was named for Achilles, who was said to have carried the plant into the battles of the Trojan War to cure his soldiers' wounds. Before there were styptic pencils, the roots of yarrow were used for many years to heal shaving cuts. The same blood-clotting effect was achieved by boiling the leaves into a salve, which led to such other common names for this plant as soldier's woundwort, nosebleed, bloodwort, staunchgrass, and staunchweed.

The yarrow has also been used to treat other ailments. Native Americans used it for burns and bruises and to cure earaches. Early American settlers chewed on the leaves to settle an upset stomach, and the women used yarrow to alleviate menstrual discomfort. Europeans chewed on the leaves to relieve toothaches and dried the leaves to make tea, which was used to treat fever, chills, gout, earaches, and headaches. Leaves ground into a salve were used for rashes and other skin irritations. At one time in Nordic countries, yarrow was used in place of hops in brewing beer.

Yarrow was sometimes placed under pillows (wrapped in flannel) in the belief that the sleeping person would dream about future loves. The Chinese believed that eating the plant brightened the eyes and increased intelligence. One unpleasant myth attached to yarrow, which was once called devil's plaything, is that it was used by Satan to cast spells.

The fernlike leaves of yarrow are quite delicate, very pretty, and aromatic when crushed. Above the leaves, flat flower clusters of white, yellow, or magenta appear in early summer and sometimes again in early fall. The common yarrow, *A. millefolium*, has white flowers and very finely cut, dark green, aromatic foliage.

The yarrow is native to Europe and western Asia but has become naturalized as a wildflower in North America, New Zealand, and Australia. It can appear in the woods, along roads, in hot, dry meadows, or on gravelly sandbanks. It is nearly impervious to drought and poor soil, and it is an excellent plant to use where soil-erosion control is needed because it has a very strong root system.

Other common yarrows include the golden yarrow, *A. filipendulina*, which differs from the common yarrow in that it has gray-green leaves and larger clusters of golden-yellow flowers. These plants are slightly hairy and can reach a height of five feet. The woolly yarrow, *A. tomentosa*, has yellow flowers that bloom over fuzzy, ground-hugging foliage.

A close relative, the golden yarrow, *Eriophyllum confleriflorum*, is also in the Daisy Family but in a different genus. The genus name, *confleriflorum*, is from the Greek word for "woolly leaf." Like the yarrow, the golden yarrow has flat-topped clusters of golden-yellow flowers, but the clusters are much smaller. The gray-green leaves are finely dissected, erect, and clasping along the stem. The woolly fuzz that densely covers the leaves and the stems was used by the Native Americans as a cure for rheumatism.

*T*histles, which are known for their sharp, prickly foliage and spiny stems that keep both wild animals and wildflower pickers away, don't look like daisies either; but like yarrow, they are members of the Daisy Family and have a number of legends associated with them. One tells of a group of Norse invaders from Denmark who, in attempting to capture a Scottish castle, walked barefoot through the moat, which had been drained of water and filled with thistle. Their cries of pain alerted the Scots, and the capture was averted. It is perhaps because of this legend that the Scots have adopted the thistle as their national emblem. Whatever the case, they have long believed that wearing thistle will protect them from harm.

The common, or bull, thistle, *Cirsium lanceolatum*, has pinkish purple tufts of flowers. It frequently grows in pastures where cattle graze (as one of its common names indicates) and has a strong root system, which contributes to its tenacity. The bull thistle's bristled seeds are carried by the wind for great distances, starting new colonies far and wide. Bull thistle can be distinguished from other purple-flowered thistles by the large "wings" that run up and down the length of the stem.

The snowy thistle, *C. pastoris*, is native to northern California, southern Oregon, and western Nevada. It is a biennial, which means that it grows the first year, forms tufts of red-tipped white flowers the second year, and then dies, dropping its seeds to grow into new plants. The spear thistle, *C. vulgare*, has a pinkish purple flower head that resembles a bottle brush emerging from a cone-shaped base.

The sale of Canada thistle, *C. arvense*, is outlawed in 37 of the United States, because it is such an aggressive plant, but it still flourishes because of its fast-creeping roots (which have given it the nickname creeping thistle) and easily spreading seeds. Its stems can grow as high as three feet and are topped with lavender flowers.

The holy or blessed thistle, *Cnicus benedictus*, is a yellow-flowered thistle, once used as a diuretic and as a cure for pleurisy. The carline thistle, *Carlina vulgaris*, is believed to be very poisonous when fresh; it has, however, been used as a treatment for tapeworms after being soaked in honey and sugar, or when dried.

The field sow thistle has flowers that resemble those of the dandelion and leaves that resemble the common thistle's. Known botanically as *Sonchus asper*, it has been eaten by humans and animals for hundreds of years. The common name stems from the fact that the field sow thistle is a favorite food of pigs: the sap is milky, and so the plant was frequently fed to female pigs to increase their milk supply. This species was also recommended for women who were nursing, for the same reason. A mixture of the leaves with wine was said to hasten childbirth.

Farmers have used field sow thistle to treat their animals for a variety of ailments including fever, heart disorders, and high blood pressure. Humans have eaten the leaves, which have little taste but lots of vitamin C, for asthma, wheezing, and shortness of breath. Men have consumed it to prolong virility. The flower seeds are fluffy and were once used in pillows and mattresses.

SNAPDRAGON/FIGWORT FAMILY

The Snapdragon Family, *Scrophulariaceae*, includes such well-loved wildflowers as Indian paintbrushes, beardtongues, mullein, and butter-and-eggs (in addition to the common garden ornamental, the snapdragon).

Indian paintbrushes, members of the *Castilleja* genus, bring bright colors to the Rocky Mountain region. There is an old legend that a Native American god gave some paintbrushes dripping with brightly colored paint to an Indian brave who was sitting on a mountainside so that he could paint the sunset. When the brave finished, he left the paintbrushes on the ground, and they grew into these delightful flowers.

The genus name for the Indian paintbrush was given in honor of Domingo Castillejo, a Spanish botanist. Despite its attractive colors, the plant is known to be a bit of a parasite, attaching itself to the roots of other plants in order to steal nutrients from them, especially when its seeds are germinating.

Native Americans used the Indian paintbrush to heal burned skin and to ease the pain of the centipede's bite. Native American women also made tea using its roots.

The true flowers of the Indian paintbrush are very small; they are surrounded by brightly colored, flowerlike, fan-shaped bracts of red, orange, yellow, and sometimes purple.

Like many other wildflowers, Indian paintbrushes are pollinated by hummingbirds and insects carrying pollen about on their heads after enjoying the flower's nectar; since the tubular flowers offer no landing place for many insects, they can be cross-pollinated only by hummingbirds or hovering insects.

There are many species of Indian paintbrush. One, *C. linariaefolia*, is the state flower of Wyoming. The scarlet Indian paintbrush, *C. coccinea*, has bright scarlet flowers; the downy Indian paintbrush, *C. sessiflora*, has green flowers; the purple Indian paintbrush, *C. purpurea*, has, of course, purple flowers; and the giant red Indian paintbrush, *C. miniata*, has red flowers.

The Indian paintbrush is magnificent in the wild but difficult to grow in cultivated gardens, because the plants do not reproduce as well. However, once a planting is established, it will withstand varying environmental conditions.

Commonly called beardtongues, the members of the *Penstemon* genus have a distinct characteristic that influences insects and birds and their ability to pollinate the flower. A prominent fifth stamen that projects from all beardtongue flowers lacks the pollen case that is found on the other four. This infertile stamen is instead covered with a fuzzy growth of hair—resembling a beard—which almost closes the throat of the flower. Because the shape of the opening, as well as the color of the flower, varies from species to species, different kinds of beardtongues attract and admit different kinds of pollinators. Several different species may grow side by side, but because of this characteristic, there is little cross-pollination between them.

The generic name for beardtongue was developed from the Greek words *pente*, meaning "five," and *stemen*, meaning "stamen," referring to the plant's five stamens. There are about 250 different beardtongues, all but two of which are native to the western part of North America; one of these is native to Central America and the other to northeastern Asia. All beardtongues have tubular flowers, which vary in size, shape, and color. Colors can be red, purple, blue, white, or yellow and attract a wide range of colorful butterflies. Most bloom in the summertime and grow best where the soil is dry and well drained and the air is cool, although penstemons with upright stems grow best in areas that have more rainfall and the low-growing, ground-hugging types flourish in areas with less precipitation.

The large-flowered beardtongue, *P. grandiflorus*, has the largest flowers of all beardtongues; they are lavender-blue and flare out at the end of the tube, exposing the fuzzy tongue. The foxglove beardtongue, *P. digitalis*, grows four to five feet tall, and, as its name suggests, the purple-tinged white flowers resemble the *Digitalis* genus's foxglove. True foxglove is the primary source of digitalis, a heart medication that today keeps many cardiac sufferers alive.

The Rocky Mountain or porch penstemon, *P. strictus*, which is a native of the western side of the Continental Divide, is especially good for erosion control on dry slopes. Its flowers are blue and bloom on only one side of the one- to three-foot stems. Flowers of this species vary in size from three-quarters of an inch to one and three quarter inches long. The variation in flower size is the product of the evolutionary interplay between the flowers and their local pollinating insects. The two lobes of the flower's upper lip project like a roof over the lower lip's three lobes, which serve as a platform for bees. It is this configuration that gives the plant its second common name, porch penstemon.

The Platte River or Wasatch penstemon, *P. cyananthus*, got its common names from the Platte River in Wyoming and the Wasatch Mountains in Utah. Its fifth, or bearded, stamen is golden yellow and is surrounded by bright blue to blue-violet petals. The showy, or royal, penstemon, *P. spectabilis*, has up to 100 flowers in a spike on the top half of the stem. The swollen flowers may be blue, violet, or pink.

*T*he mullein is another member of the Snapdragon Family. It is in the *Verbascum* genus; the common name, mullein, comes form the Latin word *mollis*, which means "soft," for the downiness of its leaves. The mullein's botanical name has the same meaning, as *verbascum* is a corruption of the Latin *barbascum*, which means "bearded." The mullein is sometimes called Quaker rouge, for it was used by young Quaker girls, who were not allowed to wear makeup to enhance their coloring.

The mullein, which has also been called Jacob's staff and shepherd's club, has been known since ancient times and was used by the Roman armies for torches. The stout stems grow two to four feet tall and when dipped in candle wax, they burn for quite a long time. At one time, the mullein was called witch's candle: those who worshipped the devil used it as a torch the same way the Roman soldiers did. Witches and warlocks supposedly used it in their brews, while others found use for it in love potions. By contrast, some considered it a powerful charm against demons. The thick down found along the stems and leaves is still used in parts of Europe to make candle wicks.

The mullein's downiness has given the plant another common name: flannel plant. It has also been called beggar's blanket, because peasants and gypsies put the leaves in their shoes to insulate their feet from the cold.

Cattlemen have called mullein cow's or bullock's lungwort, because of its use for centuries as a treatment for pulmonary congestion in cattle. Native Americans smoked the leaves for the same reason, and during the early 1900's a cough medicine made from the plant was popular. These respiratory uses are actually valid, for medical research has shown that the mullein contains agents that soothe inflamed tissue and soften the skin. Native Americans also boiled the leaves and rubbed them on body joints to relieve rheumatism, on the head to cure a headache, and on the stomach as a cure for a stomachache.

The generic name for common, or great, mullein is *V. thapsus*. It can grow to as tall as eight feet and has yellow flowers that bloom in summer in a dense spike. In Switzerland, the flower spires rise from mountainsides like golden candles, but these plants can be found throughout the temperate world. The moth mullein, *V. blattaria*, is an Old World native that has spread the temperate world over. The fuzzy stamens, which are found in the center of the white or yellow flower with spreading petals, are responsible for its common name.

*B*utter-and-eggs, *Linaria vulgaris*, has a snapdragonlike flower (not surprisingly, as it is a member of the Snapdragon Family) and is sometimes called toadflax, because the flower opens like a toad's mouth when squeezed. The reference to flax is based on the similarity of its leaves to flax leaves; this also led to its botanical name, a derivation of *Linum*, the Latin word for "flax."

A Scottish superstition as old as the thistle myth about the Norse invaders states that if a person walks in a circle around a planting of butter-and-eggs three times, any spell that has been cast upon him or her will be broken. The English believed that placing three seeds of this plant on a linen thread would protect them against evil.

The common name for butter-and-eggs stems from its two-colored flower; the two upper petals are yellow (the butter), while the three lower ones are orange (the eggs). It is sometimes called ranstead or ramstead, because it is believed to have been brought to America from Wales by a Mr. Ramstead. Other common names are dead-men's-bones and gallwort, the latter because it was included in chicken feed to rid the chickens of gallstones.

Butter-and-eggs has a slightly sweet fragrance that, to some, smells medicinal. Tea made from the leaves was used to treat jaundice and pinkeye. A salve made from the plant was used to relieve the itching of insect bites and as a base for skin lotions and ointments. The plant's juice, when mixed with milk, was used to trap flies. The arrangement of the petals on the flower, which looks like a mouth and throat, led many to believe it would be a good cure for sore throats. The color has been extracted from the flowers and used as a dye.

Butter-and-eggs was first brought to North America from Europe around 1800. The flower may look delicate, but it is not; it will grow almost anywhere. The nectar forms in a long spur, which is an indication that it is pollinated by humming-birds and long-tongued insects. As insects land on a flower, the lower petals open under their weight; the insects will then go inside for a drink of nectar and back out covered with pollen.

The spurred snapdragon, *L. maroccana,* is a close relative of butter-and-eggs and is a native of Morocco, as the species name suggests. It has delicate, long-spurred flowers of yellow and purple that are blotched in contrasting colors. *L. genistifolia,* another relative, is a perfect example of an introduced plant that was brought to North America with good intentions but became an unwelcome guest. It came from Europe after World War II and adapted quickly, but it is now a serious pest in western wheat fields because it is difficult to eradicate.

Other wildflowers in the *Linaria* genus include the cloven lip toadflax, *L. bipartita,* a native of Portugal and North Africa whose upper, violet-purple flower lip is deeply lobed; the old field toadflax, *L. canadensis,* a North American native that has tiny blue or violet-blue flowers; the striped toadflax, *L. repens,* a European wildflower that has white flowers veined in purple; the purple-net toadflax, *L. reticulata,* a western Mediterranean plant whose purple flowers are veined in a netted design; and three-birds-flying, *L. triornithophora,* which has large, pale lavender flowers striped with purple and set off by a long spur.

*O*wl's clover, *Orthocarpus purpurascens,* is not a clover at all—it is related to the snapdragon. The small rose-and-yellow or rose-and-white flowers look like owl's heads, hence the common name. Its other common name, escobite, is from a Spanish word meaning "little broom," and refers to the upright tufts of flowers and bracts, which appear at the top of one-and-one-half-foot stems covered with threadlike divided leaves. Owl's clover can be parasitic in the wild and frequently obtains nourishment from the roots of nearby grasses, although this is not among its growing requirements.

LILY FAMILY

Lily Family members, *Lilaceae,* are numerous and diverse. The family is complex, encompassing, among others, the true lily, daylily, and trillium genera. These are related to such edible and curative plants as the onion, garlic, and asparagus.

There are about 100 species of true lilies in the *Lilium* genus, as well as hundreds more outside the genus with lilylike flowers. Flowers of true lilies have six petals, which may be flaring, reflexed, or pointing forward. The flowers are oriented in different ways on the stems; some lilies have drooping flowers, others have flowers that point straight out, and still others have upward-facing flowers.

The lily is traditionally the sacred flower of motherhood. In ancient times, it was the symbol for many goddesses, in-cluding the Greek goddess Hera, who looked after a woman's marriage and childbirth, and the equivalent Roman goddess, Juno, who was responsible for the quality of women's lives.

Christian legend has it that the lily sprang from Eve's tears when she discovered that she was with child. Another says that the white lily, or Easter lily, turned white when the Virgin Mary picked it. The lily has subsequently become the Christian symbol of purity, charity, innocence, and Easter and the Resurrection.

In Puritan times, Christians removed the prominent stamens from lilies before they placed the flowers in churches, because they thought they were phallic-looking. Today, removing the stamens is still a good idea, because the yellow-orange pollen drops freely and can stain furniture and fabric.

The tiger lily, *L. tigrinum*, is one of the most easily recognized lilies, having purple-spotted orange flowers. As with some other lilies, small bulbs form along the stem where the stem meets the leaves. According to Korean legend, a hermit came upon a tiger with an arrow in its leg. The hermit removed the arrow and befriended the tiger; when the tiger later died, it was transformed into the tiger lily. When the hermit died, the tiger lily spread across the land in search of its friend.

The white Madonna lily, *L. candidum*, was once the emblem of the Greek goddess Hera and later became associated with the Virgin Mary. It is the floral emblem of Quebec and is sometimes called the Easter lily, although the lily that is most commonly referred to by this name is *L. longiflorum*, the Bermuda lily.

Canada's Saskatchewan province has chosen the wood lily, *L. philadelphicum*, as its floral emblem. This lily has orange to red upward-facing flowers with purplish-brown spots on the inside and looks somewhat like a tulip. There are gaps in the base of the petals to allow water to drain out after a rainfall. Another Canadian native wildflower is the Canada lily, or yellow meadow lily, *L. canadense*, which has nodding yellow to orange flowers. This plant is usually surrounded by buzzing bees. Its nodding habit, like that of other nodding flowers, protects the nectar from rain.

The Washington lily, *L. washingtonianum*, is a seven-foot plant with purple-dotted white flowers that may turn pink as they age. At home at altitudes of 3,000 to 7,000 feet, Washington lilies are a dramatic addition to the summer scenery from the Sierra Mountains north to Washington's Columbia River, where as many as 20 flowers per plant may be in bloom at one time. The leaves are so glossy that they look as though they are varnished.

The Turk's cap lily, *L. superbum*, its common name derived from the shape of the flower, is the largest and showiest native American lily. It grows to be eight feet tall and has as many

as 40 blooms on a plant at one time. It is sometimes known as swamp lily, a designation of its natural habitat, for it grows best in wet meadows, swamps, and bogs. Monarch butterflies are drawn to its nectar on sunny days.

Many wildflowers that are called lilies are not in the true lily, or *Lilium*, genus, but they are no less beautiful. The glacier, snow, or avalanche lily, *Erythronium grandiflorum*, brings golden tones to the Rocky Mountains in spring, with flowers with swept-back petals. The petals swing from atop a single slender stem and appear to dance against a background of foliage. The entire genus, *Erythronium*, is commonly known as trout lily, because the spotting that appears on the leaves of some of the species is similar to the markings on the fish. Two species are Eastern trout lily, *E. americanum*, which has golden-yellow flowers, and white dogtooth violet, *E. albidum*, which has white flowers and a name that describes the shape of the corm from which the plant grows. All trout lilies, whether the leaves are mottled or not, are native to moist woods, stream banks and wet meadows and bloom, coincidentally, during the spring trout season. Plants with only one leaf are considered immature; only plants with two leaves will produce flowers.

The genus name *Erythronium* comes from a Greek word meaning "red" and refers to the reddish mottling found on some species. Other names given the trout lily are fawn lily, because the two leaves stand straight up like the ears of a fawn, and adder's tongue, for the long, protruding stamens.

Trout lilies have edible leaves that can be cooked and eaten with butter as a vegetable. Roman soldiers used it on foot sores and corns, and tea brewed from the leaves has been used as a remedy for hiccups.

Mariposa lilies of the *Calochortus* genus are different from most lilies, because they have only three petals. Their common name comes from the Spanish word for "butterfly," *mariposa*, describing the gay, vivid markings on the flowers.

When the Mormons moved to Utah, their first crops failed because of insect infestations, but they kept from starving by eating the bulbs of the mariposa, which have a nutty flavor when raw and taste like potatoes when cooked. To commemorate that period, Utah chose the sego lily, *C. nuttalis*, as its state flower (*sego* is a Native American word meaning "edible bulb").

The sego lily has bowl-shaped white flowers with yellow and purple spots; the petals are fluted and slightly ruffled. Outside Utah, it is found in the Grand Canyon and much of the southwest. Other mariposa lilies with bowl-shaped flowers are the white mariposa, *C. venustus*, which has white, yellow, red, or purple flowers, usually with dark blotches on each petal, and the desert mariposa, *C. kennedyi*, which has yellow to orange flowers that have a brownish purple spot at the base of each petal.

*T*he *Brodiaea* lilies have clusters of small lilylike flowers that bloom on top of leafless stems above a few grasslike leaves. Ithuriel's spear, *B. laxa*, was named for Ithuriel, the angel in *Paradise Lost* who, with a touch of his spear, transformed Satan from a toad into his true form. This plant is also known as grassnut, because it has flavorful, bulblike corms, and is sometimes called triplet lily. The snake lily, *B. volubilis*, has purple buds and pink flowers that bloom atop a vining stalk. This plant is unique among wildflowers, because it will continue to grow and flower even if the stem is cut from the base of the plant.

The harvest lily, *B. elegans*, has violet to deep purple flowers; the pretty face, *B. lutea*, has yellow, star-shaped flowers; and the blue-dicks, or wild hyacinth, *B. pulchella*, has blue to violet flowers that bloom on red stems. Native Americans used the corm of the latter; this flower, either raw or cooked, as a source of food.

*T*he daylily is of the genus *Hemerocallis*, which is Greek for "beautiful for a day." Each lilylike flower lasts only one day but is quickly replaced by another.

Many daylily hybrids are grown in gardens, but two species remain as wildflowers: *H. lilioasphodelus*, which was once called *H. flava*, is the lemon-scented yellow daylily, an

Asian native that has become naturalized all over the world. *H. fulva*, the tawny or orange daylily, is a native of Asia and possibly Europe but also grows throughout the world. Neither of these daylily species sets seeds; they spread instead by vigorous rhizomes, which says a lot for the plants' toughness and tenacity. Daylilies start to bloom in early summer, and different varieties will bring warm tones to the cultivated garden for several months.

Newly opened daylily flowers can be boiled and buttered and served as a vegetable or dipped into batter and cooked as fritters. The tubers can also be boiled or fried and taste something like corn.

*T*he desert lily, *Hesperocallis undulata*, is a one-species genus native to the southwestern United States and Mexico. It has large white flowers with green stripes clustered at the tops of stout stems. The leaves at the base of the plant are blue-green and have wavy edges.

Native Americans of the region ate the bulbs of the desert lily and introduced them to the Spanish explorers, who liked their tangy taste, calling it *ajo*, which means "garlic." The town of Ajo, Arizona, a nearby mountain range, and a valley were all named in honor of this plant.

*T*he corn lily, or bluebeard lily, *Clintonia borealis*, was named for DeWitt Clinton, a naturalist and former governor of New York. It has yellow flowers in late spring and shiny cobalt-blue berries in the summer. Unlike those of many lilies, the leaves remain lustrous and green until midfall. Young leaves of this plant are edible and taste like cucumbers, and small animals and birds delight in eating the berries, which are not edible by humans.

*T*he Atamasco, or zephyr, lily, *Zephyranthes atamasco*, has shiny, deep green, grassy leaves and lilylike flowers of pink or white tinged with magenta. The genus name comes from the Greek words *zephyros* and *anthos*, which together mean "flower of the west wind," so named by a British botanist because the plant was brought to Europe from America—on the west wind, so to speak. The plant might also be named for Zephyrus, in Greek myth the west wind and husband to Flora, the Greek goddess of flowers. The species name, which is also one of its common names, is from a Native American word meaning "stained with red" and suggests the shading on the flowers.

Growing only 15 inches tall, the zephyr lily blooms in spring and summer in damp meadows and woods. It is also called swamp lily, fairy lily, rain lily, and Easter lily. A less appealing name is staggergrass, so given because the foliage and the bulbs are known to be poisonous.

*E*verything comes in threes in the *Trillium* genus, hence the name, which is derived from the Latin word for "three," *tres*. The leaves are in three parts, and the flowers have three petals and three sepals. The white-flowered, or large-flowered, trillium, *T. grandiflorum*, the largest flowering trillium, is sometimes called wake robin, because it is as much a harbinger of spring as the robin's red breast is. The white-flowered trillium has flowers as large as three and one-half inches across. It prefers shady locations in rich woods, but it can sometimes be found growing in drier areas in full sun.

Not all wildflowers have a delightful fragrance to attract insects and birds. The purple trillium, *T. erectum*, is sometimes called stinking Benjamin, because, as its name implies, its flowers have a foul odor, not unlike rancid meat, that attracts the carrion fly that pollinates it. Its flowers are dark red to maroon and bloom on a 16-inch stem. Ants use the coating on trillium seeds to build their nests; they discard the seeds afterwards, a unique method by which trilliums spread and reproduce.

Native Americans used trillium as a medication for the eyes, either by squeezing the juice directly into them or soaking the roots in water to make an eye wash. They also used the roots in a medication that relieved labor pains. This practice was so common that one species was named *T. ovatum* and was commonly called birthroot; it is also known as coast trillium, as it is native to moist woods along the Pacific Coast.

Native American women used trillium as an aphrodisiac to increase the amorous attentions of their mates, by boiling the root and adding it to their food. Mountain dwellers believed that if trillium was picked, it would start to rain, while some Natives Americans believed that picking the flower would bring ill fortune to an enemy.

A common trillium, the toadshade, *T. sessile*, has maroon to brown flowers and spotted leaves and can be found growing in rich woods. The plant's common name seems to be associated with its function as a hiding place for toads.

BUTTERCUP FAMILY

Members of the Buttercup Family, *Ranunculaceae*, may be beautiful, curative, or poisonous and include such diverse-looking, though familiar, flowers as the true buttercups, columbines, anemones, and marsh marigolds.

People have always been drawn to buttercups. The belief is that if the yellow buttercup is held up to one's chin and the yellow color is reflected, the holder of the flower likes butter. Members of the *Ranunculus* genus, buttercups have many myths associated with them. People once called them crazy weed and thought they caused lunacy, especially when they were held near the neck during a full moon.

The buttercup's power to drive someone crazy has certainly never been proven, but some species do cause skin irritation and blisters. Beggars once used the tall, or meadow, buttercup, *R. acris*, and cursed crowfoot, *R. sceleratus*, to induce sores on their bodies and faces to arouse sympathy. One species was used to make poison arrows. Stomach inflammation of both animals and humans occurs if fresh buttercups are ingested, and cows that eat the flowers produce bitter milk with a red tinge. Once dried, however, buttercups are generally harmless.

The genus name *Ranunculus* means "little frog" in Latin. This name may have been given because most buttercups grow in moist or boggy areas or, possibly, because the seeds resemble small frogs. The name *buttercup* refers to the color and shape of the flower.

There are over 300 species of buttercups: some grow on land, some in the water, but most in the marshy areas in between. Their yellow flowers are waxy, and their spreading, usually divided leaves have given them the common name of crowfoot. They are very pretty in a wildflower bouquet with clovers and daisies, a combination giving off a sweet meadow scent.

In addition to the meadow buttercup, which has glossy yellow petals on a slightly hairy plant, one of the other most common buttercups is bulbous buttercup, *R. bulbosus*, which has a distinct swelling at the base of the stem. Creeping buttercup, *R. repens*, creeps along the ground in damp woods, where its deep yellow flowers stand out against the contrasting background. The lesser celandine, *R. ficaria*, looks less like a buttercup than the others: the flowers are starlike, with narrower petals, and the leaves are undivided and heart-shaped. The lesser celandine bears no relationship to the greater celandine, *Chelidonium majus*, which is in the Poppy Family.

Water crowfoots have the same flower structure as the buttercup, but their flowers are white. They are totally or almost totally aquatic plants. The common water crowfoot, *R. aquatilis*, has both rounded, floating leaves and divided, submerged ones. The flowers are almost an inch across and have a green spot at the base of the petals. The river water crowfoot, *R. fluitans*, is found only in running water and usually lacks floating leaves. The ivy-leaves water crowfoot, *R. hederaceus*, has rounded, ivylike leaves and grows in mud rather than water.

*B*uttercups are close relatives of marsh marigolds, *Caltha palustris*, which actually bear little resemblance to marigolds except in color. The name *marigold* was often applied to plants with golden-yellow flowers and was derived from the words "Mary's gold"; marigold flowers were placed on altars during religious ceremonies. The marsh marigold is sometimes known as cowslip, a name also applied to Virginia bluebells and to one primrose, *Primula veris*. Its common name denotes its natural habitat: marshes, swamps, and streams.

Although the marsh marigold is toxic, repeated boiling makes the plant edible, and, in fact, it was once used medicinally. The leaves contain large amounts of iron and were used to treat anemia. Flower buds were boiled, sautéed, or

pickled and used in place of capers, and the flowers were used in medieval times to make wine, potions, and brews. Rubbing leaves on insect bites and bee stings was once practiced to relieve pain and itching.

The marsh marigold's scientific name comes from the Latin *caltha*, meaning "cup," and *palus*, meaning "marsh." The flowers grow from thick roots that produce stout, hollow stems with broad, heart-shaped leaves. After the flowers fade, the leaves increase in size. The flowers, which have five glossy yellow petal-like sepals and a cluster of prominent stamens, are a sign that spring has settled.

The elkslip, *C. leptosepala*, is often eaten without harm by moose and elk. It has a white flower with a yellow center and heart-shaped leaves that are clustered at the base of the plant.

*C*olumbines, *Aquilegia*, are also members of the Buttercup Family, although less obviously so; their five petals stretch back to form spurs where nectar collects. The flowers bloom in late spring and early summer, nodding from the tops of their stems, with spurs pointing upwards. All of the columbines native to the New World are pollinated by hummingbirds; Old World species are pollinated by long-tongued moths. Bumblebees are known to pierce the spurs and steal the nectar of columbines, but they usually do so without pollinating the flower.

The genus name *Aquilegia* is from the Latin word for "eagle," so named because the spurs resemble an eagle's claws. The word *columbine* is taken from the Latin word *columbinus*, meaning "dovelike," as the spurs often resemble a circle of dove's heads.

Columbines grow naturally on mountainsides, in semi-dry, open areas and at the edge of woodlands. They are long-lasting flowers, both in the wild and in cut-flower arrangements. They have long been the symbol of a deserted lover, so it is considered an insult to give one to a woman and bad luck to give it to a man.

In ancient times, columbines were used medicinally. The sap from fresh plants was used to treat jaundice, intestinal pain, and swelling of the liver. The plant was supposedly used to cure measles and smallpox, and one legend tells of lions that ate columbines to increase their strength.

Flowers of the North Temperate Zone, columbines are

sometimes called *gants de Notre Dame*, meaning "Our Lady's gloves," referring to the five spurs that look like fingers in a glove. The garden columbine, *A. vulgaris*, has hooked rather than straight spurs and is, therefore, called crow's foot. Introduced into North America from Europe, it has small white, violet, or pink blooms. Other common names for the columbine are meeting house, because the five spurs suggest a committee meeting with the members sitting in a circle around a table, and rock bells, for the bell-shaped flowers bloom wildly in the Rocky Mountains, the Alps, and similarly mountainous environments.

Columbine flowers are sometimes solid-colored and sometimes two-toned; all bloom on slender stems above divided foliage. The wild or eastern columbine, *A. canadensis*, has red and yellow flowers, while the state flower of Colorado, known variously as the Rocky Mountain, Colorado, or blue columbine, *A. caerulea*, has blue-and-white flowers. The longspur columbine, *A. longissima*, has yellow flowers with spurs as long as eight inches. The scarlet or Sitke columbine, *A. formosa*, has bright red blooms.

*A*nother plant in the Buttercup Family whose name is a derivation of a Greek word is *Anemone*, or windflower, from the name of the Greek goddess of the wind, Anemos. How the plant became associated with wind is not exactly known, but it has been suggested that it is because the plants bloom in early spring when the wind still howls; Pliny wrote that only the wind could open the anemone's flowers. The name has also been linked to the wind that constantly blows on Mount Olympus, the Mountain of the Gods, where anemones once grew wild. And yet another theory attributes the wildflower's name to its fluffy seed heads, which are easily blown about in the breeze.

An ancient legend tells of the anemones that grew where Venus shed her tears after the death of her lover, Adonis. The Romans picked anemones in the spring, all the while chanting, in the belief that this would guard against illness in the coming year.

Other cultures treated the anemone quite differently. In the Near East, people thought anemones caused sickness and would neither go near them nor breathe the air where they grew. The Chinese planted the anemone in cemeteries and

called it the death plant.

A wildflower in the *Anemone* genus is the Pasque flower, *A. pulsatilla*, which blooms in early spring during the Pasque season, that is, Passover and Easter—hence its name. Native Americans regarded it as a herald of spring and, because of its shaggy heads of feathery seeds, a sign of old age. The flowers bloom within a silky, furlike covering that protects them from the cold. The appearance of the shaggy seed head has also given Pasque flower the name prairie smoke. It is the state flower of South Dakota and the floral emblem of the Province of Manitoba, Canada.

The wood anemone, *A. quinquefolia*, blooms along rich woodland borders, in thickets, and in wet meadows in early spring, its white flowers blooming before the whorls of divided and toothed leaves appear. Actually, the flower has no petals but is instead made up of petal-like sepals, a characteristic of all anemones. After the flowers fade, the leaves will disappear, but the roots remain active, creeping underground to increase the size of the colony the following year.

Both the Pasque flower and wood anemone are low-growing plants, and their flowers are borne on short, hairy stalks until they are pollinated by crawling insects. After the seeds form, the stalks grow several more inches so the seeds can be captured by the breeze.

Some anemones are tall-growing and are pollinated by bees and other flying insects. The taller anemones include the western anemone, *A. occidentalis*, which has creamy white flowers and seed heads covered with long white hairs; because of these characteristics, it is one of several wildflowers to be called old man of the mountain. The thimbleweed, *A. cylindrica*, has small white flowers, but it is more easily recognized by the cylindrical, or thimblelike, seed heads. Another anemone commonly called thimbleweed is *A. virginiana*. It is a three-foot plant with inconspicuous flowers but, like *A. cylindrica*, it has large, thimblelike seed heads that can be dried and dyed for use in cut-flower arrangements.

The Canada anemone, *A. canadensis*, has white flowers that bloom in late spring or summer and are followed by a burrlike cluster of seeds. The root system is extensive and the roots were used by Native Americans for medicinal purposes. This anemone is one of the easiest northeastern North American wildflowers to grow in a home garden.

The rue anemone, known botanically as *Anemonella thalictroides*, is not a true anemone. The plants, however, look a lot like anemones, growing eight inches tall, with divided leaves and pink or white daisylike flowers. Since they are anemone look-alikes, they are called *Anemonella*, or little anemones. The rue anemone was adopted by the Persians as a symbol of disease. At one time, the plant was thought to have great healing powers, but now it is used only occasionally, to treat foot disorders.

CARROT FAMILY

Carrot Family members, *Apiaceae*, grow mostly in the Northern Hemisphere and in their cultivated forms include carrots, parsnips, celery, coriander, parsley, and dill, to name a few.

Summer fields and roadsides are filled with the swaying stems and fernlike foliage of Queen Anne's lace, *Daucus carota*, also known as wild carrot.

When Anne became Queen of England, she challenged her ladies-in-waiting to make a lace as beautiful as the plants in her garden. A respected tatter herself, she naturally won the contest, for nobody would dare to outdo a queen. Of course, her name was given to the plant and it is still known as Queen Anne's lace. It was brought to North America by early settlers to remind them of their homeland.

Queen Anne's lace has a four-to five-foot stem that becomes soft and flexible during wet weather, so that the flower head bends down and the pollen is protected from the rain. Older plants that have already been pollinated will stand up straight, even during heavy storms. Queen Anne's lace has a strong aroma that insects love—the golden swallowtail butterfly is a frequent visitor—but that many people find disagreeable. The seed heads are somewhat spiny and are shaped like a bird's nest filled with tangled wool, which has given rise to another common name, bird's nest.

A native of Afghanistan, Queen Anne's lace has been used for its medicinal qualities. Grated roots contain a substance called carotin, a good remedy for burns, and both the roots and juice from the stems have been used for combating internal parasites.

Although the root of Queen Anne's lace, like the carrot, is edible, there is danger of confusing the plant with its look-alike cousins, poison hemlock, *Conicum maculatum*, and water hemlock, *Cicuta maculata*, so great care must be taken when gathering plants from the wild for food. The center of the Queen Anne's lace flower head usually has one dark purple or red flower, which can help in identification. There is a legend that Queen Anne pricked her finger when making her lace and that a single drop of blood fell to color the center of the flower. It was once believed that eating this part of the flower would cure epilepsy.

Also in the carrot family is the sea holly, *Eryngium maritinum*. It grows along beaches and sand dunes and has bright blue-green leaves that are thickly edged with spiny teeth. The flowers are purple or electric blue and bloom in rounded heads containing many spines.

The sea holly is related to the rattlesnake master or button snakeroot, *E. yuccifolium*. "Rattlesnake master" is somewhat of a misnomer, because the plant has no proven medicinal value for treating snakebites and looks nothing like a rattlesnake. The leaves are stiff, with spiny edges, and Native Americans used fibers from them to make rope. The greenish white flowers bloom in clusters.

PEA FAMILY

The Pea Family members, *Fabaceae*, include clover, bluebonnets, and false indigo. The Pea Family enriches the soil it grows in, unlike other plants that use up their soil, by "fixing" nitrogen into it.

Humankind has searched many a summer meadow in search of four-leaved clovers, which are regarded as a symbol of good luck. They may have found enjoyment, but success has usually been limited, as most clovers in the *Trifolium* genus have only three leaves (or more correctly, leaflets). Three-leaved clovers have long been regarded as a symbol of fertility, domestic virtue, and the Holy Trinity.

The clover provides the perfect example of the relationship between plants and the insect world. Without insects, which these plants absolutely need, there would be little pollination, no seeds, and, therefore, no more new plants. When the Australians first imported seeds of red clover to grow plants as cattle forage, they had no success, for they forgot to import bumblebees to pollinate the plants; bumblebees are about the only insects that visit clover.

The clover was brought to the United States also as a forage plant, but it soon became an escaped wildflower. The flowers were once used in cough medicine, and teas were made to improve the strength of finger- and toenails and to purify the blood. The flowers were also used to make wine, flavor tobacco and cheese, cure athlete's foot, and repel moths. The roots, stems, and leaves are also edible. Because the clover fixes nitrogen in the soil, it is a useful cover crop. Honey made from clover is among the tastiest, and it is a tasty treat to suck the sweet nectar from the flowers' bases, as is done with honeysuckle flowers.

All clovers are summer-blooming plants. The red clover, *T. pratense*, is the state flower of Vermont. It has dense, rounded heads of pink flowers and pointed leaflets. The white, or Dutch, clover, *T. repens*, is a lower-growing plant that has pink-based white flowers and heart-shaped leaflets. It is a common pasture plant, often sown with mixtures of grasses. The rabbit's foot clover, *T. arvense*, has white flowers hidden by soft pink to tan wool that covers its oval head. This clover is an annual and may disappear during the heat of a very dry summer, leaving its seeds to grow the following spring. While it is in bloom, its soft, fuzzy flowers are appealing to look at and touch and have a sweet scent.

The hop clover, sometimes called yellow clover, *T. agrarium*, hails from Europe and Asia Minor but is now a wildflower found across North America. *Agrarium* means "of fields" in Latin—fields being the plant's natural habitat. The hop clover's fresh blooms are soft and pleasant to the touch. As the dense yellow flowers wither, they turn brown and fold downward, resembling dried hops.

A close cousin to the clover is the prairie clover, in the genus *Petalostemum*. Its conical flowers are somewhat larger than those of the clover; flowering begins at the bottom of the cone and proceeds upward in a ring. High in protein and good for grazing animals, the prairie clover has either bright magenta flowers, *P. purpureum*, or white flowers, *P. candidum*. These plants have deep root systems and can therefore survive periods of long drought; the roots have been used in tea, which was said to reduce fever. Many farmers prefer the prairie clover as forage over the white clover, because it is not as aggressive and does not attract as many rabbits.

The bush clovers, *Lespedeza*, are native to eastern North America, east Asia, and Australia. Like other clovers, they are grown in pastures for grazing, are used to make hay, and are excellent soil improvers. The seeds of some species are a primary food for quail. The round-headed bush clover, *L. capitata*, has bristly clusters of cream-colored flowers with red to brown markings.

The sweet clover, like the true clover, was brought to North America from the Old World to be grown in pastures, as cover crops, and for honey. It is the fragrance of sweet clover that most people associate with country hay. There are two common types: *Melilotus alba*, white sweet clover, a bushy plant with spikes of white flowers that can reach heights of one to eight feet, and the shorter yellow sweet clover, *M. officinalis*.

The Irish shamrock, *Trifolium procumbens*, is in fact a clover; the intersections on modern highways and freeways have been called cloverleaves to describe their shamrocklike design.

*A*s a result of the efforts of former First Lady "Lady Bird" Johnson, more than a million miles of Texas roadside have been planted with wildflowers, primarily the Texas bluebonnet.

The Texas bluebonnet is a member of the *Lupinus* genus. The word *lupine* comes from the Latin word *lupus*, which means "wolf." It was once believed that the lupine robbed the soil of its richness, just as the wolf robbed the shepherd of sheep, or that the lupine "wolfed" nutrients from the soil. Actually, just the opposite is true, because lupines are legumes, like peas, beans, and clover, and are capable of taking nitrogen from the air and fixing it into the soil. Because of this, they thrive in poor soil, making their own fertilizer. Texas bluebonnets grow one to two feet tall with spikes of blue flowers that bloom in late spring.

Texas bluebonnets, *Lupinus subcarnosus* or *L. texensis,* have many relatives in the wildflower world. Far north of Texas, the bluish purple blooms of *L. latifolius subalpinus* cover the cold Alaskan mountains. From Maine to Florida, the wild lupine or blue lupine, *L. perennis,* fills mid-to late-spring gardens with spires of blue pealike flowers; it is one of the few lupines that grows wild in the eastern United States. Another, the white lupine or field lupine, *L. albus,* is a four-foot annual, unlike most lupines, which are perennials.

Beautiful yellow flowers grace summer fields when the golden lupine, *L. densiflorus,* is in bloom. The arroyo lupine, or succulent lupine, *L. succulentus,* is a purple-flowered annual that grows with moderate amounts of water, despite the implication from its name that it is a desert plant. It is also called purple annual lupine to describe the flowers; another name, succulent lupine, describes the thick stem.

Texas bluebonnets and other lupines have leaves arranged like the fingers on a hand; these leaves follow the sun and close at night to retain heat and conserve moisture. For this reason, lupines are sometimes called sundial plants.

*L*upines are close relatives of false indigo, members of the *Baptisia* genus. They are named false indigo because they contain a blue dye that resembles indigo. False indigo's generic name is derived from the Greek word *baptizein,* which means "to dye." When the sap is dried and exposed to air, it turns purple. Like the true indigo, *Indigofera tinctoria,* the false indigo is a legume.

Most false indigos, the most common of which is *B. australis,* have, as the word *indigo* suggests, blue or purple flowers. The species name *australis* really has nothing to do with Australia; it is from the Greek word for "southern" and is used to denote the origin of the plants, which are native to the southern United States. The common false indigo has bluish green cloverlike leaves and spikes of blue flowers that bloom in early summer on bushy plants. The seed pods can be picked and dried before they ripen and used in winter flower arrangements. Some false indigo species exhibit lighter-colored flowers: prairie false indigo, *Baptisia leucantha,* has white flowers, and yellow wild indigo or yellow rattleweed, *B. tinctoria,* has yellow blooms.

In addition to using it for dye, the colonists found another use for the false indigo: they placed it in harnesses and used it to brush away horseflies while farming, hence its common names—horsefly weed, horseweed, and shoofly. Although the leaves resemble clover, and many of its close relatives are edible, the false indigo is not.

BLUEBELL FAMILY

Members of the Bluebell Family, *Campanulaceae,* grow in both tropical and temperate regions. The family includes all the bellflowers and lobelia and is often "tamed" for garden use.

The bellflowers of the *Campanula* genus are a varied lot whose common denominator is a bell-shaped or star-shaped flower, usually blue but sometimes pink or white. The generic name is the Latin word for "little bell." California bluebells, *C. prenanthoides,* are among the most unusual, as the style (the central portion of the flower that is part of its female reproductive system) extends beyond the flower for at least twice the flower's length.

The harebell, *C. rotundifolia,* may have been named because of its association with witches, who were believed to be able to use this plant to transform themselves into hares that would bring a person bad luck. In Scotland, bellflowers were once called witches' thimbles. Another, more ordinary, reason for the name is that the harebell grows in areas where hares live, from sea level to one mile above, in open fields and meadows. The harebell has blue to lavender flowers that bloom in summer on thin, hairlike stems with round leaves.

The southern harebell, *C. divaricata,* is taller than *C. rotundifolia,* reaching three feet in height. Its blue flowers are very tiny and the edges of the petals are upturned. Like the California bluebell, it has a protruding style. The creeping bellflower, *C. rapunculoides,* gets its name from the creeping habit of the rhizomes (root system). The plants have nodding purple flowers that open along a narrow spiked stem.

One of the largest bellflowers is the tall, or American, bellflower, *C. americana,* which can reach seven feet in height and has star-shaped blue flowers that appear along the stems at the base of the leaves. While many bellflowers are native to dry areas, tall harebells grow in moist woods and thickets. The original Canterbury Bells of Elizabethan botanists were called

C. trachelium, a tall plant with hairy toothed leaves and narrow flowers; the name Canterbury Bells is now applied to a different bellflower, *C. medium*.

One of the wonders of wildflowers is their interaction with the rest of the natural world. The bright red late-summer blooms of the cardinal flower, *Lobelia cardinalis*, attract hummingbirds, especially in early morning and at dusk. The birds carry pollen on their heads from one flower to another as they drink the nectar. Most insects cannot reach inside the long, tubular blooms of the cardinal flower, and bumblebees find the flowers too light to rest upon, so the hummingbird is its only source of pollination. Cardinal flowers have no fragrance; it is the color that attracts the birds. Other members of the genus are pollinated by bees or butterflies.

The *Lobelia* genus is a varied one. Some species are annual, some perennial, with plants ranging in height from several inches to nearly 30 feet. All of the flowers are tubular and divided into two lips—the upper lip has two lobes, and the lower one has three. All members of the genus prefer partial shade and moist soil.

Cardinal flowers were one of the first plants sent from the Americas to Europe, as early as 1626. The genus was named after the Flemish botanist Matthias de l'Obel, who was the physician to King James I in the early seventeenth century. The common name comes from the color of the flower, the same color worn by cardinals of the Roman Catholic Church, and was supposedly given to the plant by Queen Henrietta Maria of England. The cardinal flower is one of the few red-flowered plants in a genus whose members have mostly blue flowers.

The roots of the cardinal flower were once considered to be a powerful love charm and were believed to make a person amorous if used as a body lotion. Livestock avoid the cardinal flower, because they do not like its taste—which is just as well, as the plants can be toxic. Native Americans boiled the roots and used the tea to cure intestinal worms; the stems and leaves of Indian tobacco, or pukeweed, *L. inflata*, which contain a chemical known as lobeline, are still used as an emetic and as a treatment for bronchial and pulmonary diseases.

The roots of the great blue lobelia, *L. siphilitica*, have been used as a remedy for syphilis and other diseases. Sometimes called blue cardinal flower, it has spikes of blue flowers. The spiked lobelia, *L. spicata*, also has blue flowers, but it is taller than the three-foot great blue lobelia and a bit lighter in color. The great blue lobelia blooms in late summer, while the spiked lobelia blooms earlier in the season.

VIOLET FAMILY

The Violet Family, *Violaceae*, is perhaps one of the showiest and certainly one of the best-known of all wildflower families. Songs have touted the sweet fragrance of violets, "sweeter than all the roses," and bouquets of violets have long been used to try to win over an undecided heart. Shakespeare often wrote about violets, extolling them for their constancy and using them in his work as a symbol of love.

The violet is steeped in wildflower mythology. One legend tells that Zeus was in love with a nymph named Io and that to hide her from his wife, Hera, he changed her into a heifer. Io, which is the Greek word for violet, did not like the pasture grasses she had to eat and started to cry. Zeus, feeling penitent, changed the grasses into more tasty violets. Another version of the story says that Hera did in fact discover Zeus's feelings towards Io and that it was Hera who changed Io into a heifer, and yet another version says that violets were created to honor Io for her beauty.

Ancient Roman women mixed violets with goat's milk and used the solution as a facial cream. The ancient Romans also used it to strengthen the heart, to calm a bad temper, and as a sleeping potion. It was thought by the Romans that wearing a garland of violets would prevent drunkenness, although all it probably did was mask the odor of alcohol.

Much later in history, Napoleon Bonaparte promised to return to France from exile when the violets bloomed in the spring. (He always liked to have small bunches of violets on his desk when they were in season.) He kept his promise, arriving in Paris on March 20, 1815, and his followers adopted the violet as their symbol.

There are at least 500 species of violets, native to all areas of the temperate world, and different species have been chosen as the state flowers of Illinois, New Jersey, Rhode Island, and Wisconsin. Most violets have five petals, the lower one having a hollow spur and a wide area on which insects can land. Since the spur points upward, bees must back in to reach the nectar.

Many violets are indeed violet-colored, but some are blue, white, or yellow. The better the soil conditions, the more blooms a plant will produce, a characteristic used by some to determine a soil's richness. Violets grow best in light shade and moist, rich soil, although they will invade sunny, dry places as well.

The flower of the common blue violet, *Viola sororia*, is edible, as are the flowers of many other violets. It is often sugar-coated and eaten as candy, used as decorations on cakes, or floated on drinks. The flowers have also been used in jams and jellies, to make wine, and to make an herbal tea that is thought to be good for a headache. The leaves of many violets are high in vitamins A and C and are used fresh in salads. When they are cooked, they take on the consistency of okra, and they have been used in soups and sauces as a thickening agent. Some violets have been made into a syrup and used to treat stomach upset or to reduce swelling.

At one time, common blue violet was called *V. papilionacea*, the species name meaning "violet shaped like a butterfly," to describe the shape of the flowers. This violet is unique, because it produces two types of flowers. In early spring, the flowers have five petals and are similar to other violets' blooms; the bottom petal is striped with purple to guide the pollinating insects to the nectar. In late spring and summer, petalless flowers form under the leaves. These flowers produce seeds without the aid of insects. The seeds are dispersed by the explosive popping of the seed capsule or by ants who carry them to their nests, remove the outer coating, and leave them behind to grow.

A number of violets possess heart-shaped leaves, including the Canada violet, *V. canadensis*, which grows wild in forests and along stream banks. Its flowers are white with a blue-violet tint. The downy yellow violet, *V. pubescens*, has yellow flowers and leaves and stems that are covered with fine, soft hairs. The white violet, *V. macloskeyi*, has white flowers veined in maroon. The leaves of the hairy violet, *V. hirta*, are indeed hairy; the scentless flowers are pale blue-violet and have prominent orange stamens. The sweet violet, *V. odorata*, is similar to the hairy violet, but the flowers are larger and deliciously scented.

Heart-shaped leaves, however, are not characteristic of all violets. The arrowleaf violet, *V. sagittata*, has toothed leaves that are shaped like arrowheads; the small purple flowers have white centers. The lanceleaf violet, *V. lanceolata*, has long, narrow leaves and white flowers whose lower petals are veined in maroon. The yellow prairie violet, *V. nuttallii*, has yellow flowers and broad, oblong leaves.

According to a Greek legend, the Johnny-jump-up was pure white until it was wounded by one of Cupid's arrows and turned purple and yellow, like a black-and-blue mark. The Johnny-jump-up, *V. tricolor*, is native to the Pyrenees but can now be found growing throughout the temperate world. Its tufted plants have perky flowers with faces of purple, yellow, and white. Johnny-jump-up is known by a number of other common names including European wild pansy, field pansy, and miniature pansy; it is one of the parents of today's garden pansy, *V. X wittrockiana*. The other parent of the garden pansy is *V. lutea*, a European violet that may be all yellow, all purple, or a combination of the two colors.

MILKWEED FAMILY

Milkweeds, in the family *Asclepiadaceae*, comprise about 200 species; many are in the *Asclepias* genus, a name derived from Aesculapius, the Greek god of medicine. Like the Turk's cap lily, the milkweed attracts monarch butterflies, for the larvae feed on the plants.

A legend of the Old West tells about a small-framed outlaw who drank the venom of a rattlesnake every morning, building up a resistance to the toxin, so he could kill a larger man by spitting in his eye. Monarch butterflies have, in the same way, built up a resistance to the leaves of the milkweed, which are poisonous to most animals. As a result, the caterpillars and butterflies that feed on the leaves are toxic to most of their predators.

There is no medicinal value connected with milkweeds today, but at one time they were used extensively as a medicinal herb. The Quebec tribe of Canada used the roots as a contraceptive, and the United States' Shawnee tribe used the white sap of the plant to remove warts. The root was also chewed for dysentery, and the dried leaves were smoked for relief of asthma and coughing. One species was even used to treat syphilis.

The common name for milkweed comes from the white, milky juice in the stems. At one time, scientists tried to make rubber from the sap, but the project was abandoned because it was impractical and expensive. The juice protects the plants from ants, because when their feet puncture the stem, they get caught in the sticky sap. The strong, fibrous parts of the milkweed plant are used to make string or cord.

The milkweed's tiny fragrant flowers form in clusters that bloom in summer or fall. The petals are slippery, and when they are visited by bees and other insects, which have to scramble to get a footing, the pollen easily coats the insects' bodies and is carried to the next flower. The pollination process is a complicated one, which might explain why the milkweed plant contains so few seed pods but why each pod has hundreds of seeds. Only the orchid has a more complicated pollination process. The oblong seed pods form in the fall and burst open suddenly, spewing long, silky, parachuted seeds, which goldfinches use to line their nests. The seeds glisten in the sun and are beautiful.

There are 1,900 species of milkweeds. The common milkweed, *A. syriaca*, has pink to lavender flowers that are among the most fragrant of wildflowers. It is a common sight in fields and meadows during the summer. Other milkweeds are the sand or blunt-leaved milkweed, *A. amplexicaulis*, with purple to green flowers and seed pods that are long, slim, and twisted in such a way that they resemble a heron; the desert milkweed, *A. erosa*, with greenish yellow flowers; the whorled milkweed, *A. verticillata*, with white flowers; and the swamp milkweed, *A. incarnata*, with pink to violet flowers.

The sunset flower, *A. curassavica*, is sometimes called bloodflower, for the color of its blossoms. Probably native to South America, it now grows from the Southern Hemisphere to the Northern Hemisphere, and attracts hummingbirds and butterflies.

A close relative of the milkweed is the butterfly weed, *A. tuberosa*, whose bright orange flowers have been used as a dye. It is one of the few members of the milkweed genus that does not have a milky sap. Early settlers in America believed the root would cure pleurisy, which it does not, but the plant came to be known as pleurisy root anyway. Native Americans also used the roots medicinally, but today it is believed that they have no real healing value. The plants were once called chigger weed, because it was thought that they harbored great numbers of chiggers; there may have been chiggers present, but no more than on any other wildflower.

The seeds of the butterfly weed are soft and downy and were at one time used to stuff beds and cushions. The flowers are excellent as long-lasting cut flowers or as dried flowers, and the seed pods are used in dried-flower arrangements. The butterfly weed's deep tap root protects the plant from annihilation by drought, animals, wildflower fanciers, and fire.

PURSLANE FAMILY

Two great American explorers, Meriwether Lewis and William Clark, have been honored by having a wildflower named for each of them. The bitterroot, *Lewisia rediviva*, is a member of the Purslane Family, *Portulacaceae*, and a relative of the garden ornamental portulaca. It is a low-growing plant with large, showy white or pink flowers and a rosette of narrow, succulent leaves that disappear as the flowers bloom. The bitterroot grows wild in dry and rocky soil, and it was in this type of environment that Lewis first discovered the plant in the Bitterroot Valley of western Montana. Later, what are now the Bitterroot Mountains and the Bitterroot River were also named for this plant, which became the state flower of Montana.

The bitterroot's common name comes from the flavor of its bitter, fleshy root, although the bitterness disappears after the root is cooked. Harvested in spring before the plant flowers, the root can be boiled, baked, or grated; it was a staple of the Native Americans, and the early settlers came to like it too.

The bitterroot is also known as resurrection lily, because it has an amazing ability to rejuvenate after being dried out for a long period of time: with a good soaking, a plant that has been dried out for over a year can sometimes be revived. In fact, after Lewis discovered the plant in 1806 near the present site of Missoula, Montana, he dried a specimen of it; several years later, it was reported that a Mr. M'Mahon of Philadelphia planted the dried specimen and it returned to life. The bitterroot thrives irrespective of extremes and has endured winters as cold as −30° F or as warm as 40° F. Coincidentally, the species name means "restored to life."

EVENING PRIMROSE FAMILY

The clarkia, like fuchsia and fireweed, is a member of the Evening Primrose Family, *Onagraceae*. Originally native to wet areas, the clarkia is now a plant of dry regions. The *Clarkia* genus is an interesting one to botanists because of the speed with which new species are being formed and are adapting to changes in the environment. Although some species died out as the plant moved into more arid areas, new forms developed and spread out. Clarkias (the common name is the same as the genus name) prefer summer temperatures under 80° F and full sun.

Native to coastal California and Oregon, the clarkia was discovered by William Clark while he and Meriwether Lewis were exploring the Louisiana Territory. It was not long before the clarkia was introduced into Europe as a garden flower. It is an annual, rejuvenating itself each year from seeds that drop from the previous year's flowers.

One of the clarkias, *C. amoena*, is known as farewell-to-spring, because the plant comes into bloom in late spring and early summer. Other common names for it are herald-of-summer and summer's darling. It has four flat to fan-shaped petals of pink or white that are often blotched with red. The flowers usually open during the day and close during cloudy weather or at night. New hybrids with double flowers have been developed, but it's still hard to beat the simple beauty of the single-flowered original forms. The seeds of farewell-to-spring were once gathered by Native Americans for food.

Winecup clarkia, *C. purpurea*, has cup-shaped purple, lavender, or red flowers that often have dark blotches and appear in midspring. Deerhorn, *C. pulchella*, has pink to purple elaborately lobed petals that somewhat resemble an antler and bloom in summer. *C. concinna*, a California native, is commonly called red ribbons, because its bright pink to red petals are very deeply cut.

*T*he *Oenothera* genus is also an interesting one, containing two distinct types of flowers with opposite characteristics. The genus name is from a Greek word meaning "wine-imbibing," as the plant supposedly increased one's desire for alcohol. It must have been one of the first plants taken to Europe by the early American explorers, because it was known in Europe before 1600. It has also been called king's cure-all, sand lily, and German rampion.

The first type of flower in the *Oenothera* genus, the evening primrose (which has no relationship to the primrose, except that some of the species have a scent similar to primroses), has golden-yellow, pink, or white flowers that open in late afternoon and stay open until the following day. The sundrop, another type, has yellow flowers that open in the morning and close in the afternoon.

There are practical reasons why some plants open only during the day, while others open at night. Some flowers are pollinated by bees and other insects that fly mainly during sunlight hours; at night, the petals close to protect the reproductive center of the flower from rain, wind, and dust. Other plants are pollinated by such insects as night-flying moths, so they open only after dark. Most of these plants have light-colored flowers in order to show up well in the dark, making them easy to find. They are usually solid in color, as bright contrasts do little to attract insects at night.

The evening primrose, which attracts a large number of night-flying moths, got its name not only because it opens in the evening, but also because its lemony fragrance increases at that time, helping to attract pollinating insects. The flowers last only one day but may stay open a second morning for a short time if they were not pollinated the night before, in an effort to attract day-flying insects to do the job. The evening primrose has a strong root system that makes the plant aggressive and resistant to fire and drought. The roots of young plants are edible and may be used in soups and stews, to add flavor resembling that of the parsnip; the leaves can be added to salads.

The most common evening primrose is *O. biennis*, a plant with clusters of lemon-scented bright yellow flowers that bloom atop hairy reddish stems with basal, often reddish leaves. The Missouri evening primrose, *O. missouriensis*, is lower-growing with yellow flowers borne singly atop its basal leaves. The showy evening primrose, *O. speciosa*, has flowers ranging from pink to white and may be either an erect plant or a sprawling ground cover. Its name is quite a misnomer, as it is day-blooming.

The prairie evening primrose, *O. albicaulis*, has white flowers that age to pink and upper leaves that are deeply lobed. Its lovely fragrant flowers stretch over the sandy prairies of the western part of North America, and from a distance they resemble wild roses. After the flowers are pollinated, they change in color from white, to pink, to red. The beach evening primrose, *O. cheiranthifolia*, should probably be called beach sundrop, for the yellow flowers of this Oregon coast native are open only during the day.

The gumbo lily, *O. caespitosa*, has large flowers made up of heart-shaped petals. It blooms so quickly in the afternoon that the process resembles a time-lapse movie. The annual *O. lamarckiana* tolerates partial shade, alkaline soil, and drought. It is also less invasive than many other evening primroses, which can quickly take over a wildflower garden. Both flowers are native to dry prairies, fields, and wastelands.

The white evening primrose, *O. pallida*, has large, white fragrant flowers that are sometimes tinged with lilac. It forms large clumps, binds the soil well, and is tolerant of salt spray, so it is an excellent plant for beaches and dunes. The largest and showiest of the evening primroses, *O. hookeri*, commonly known as Hooker's evening primrose or giant evening prim-rose, has bright yellow flowers atop five-foot stems. These evening primroses are also both found in dry prairies, fields, and wastelands.

GENTIAN FAMILY

Gentians are another family of wildflowers, *Gentianaceae*, whose flowers have varying characteristics. The fringed gentians are members of the *Gentianopsis* genus (once called *Gentiana crinita*); they have pretty blue flowers with four fringed petals that are open during the day to reveal a white center. The closed gentian, which has several species in the *Gentiana* genus, has a different habit. The flowers have five petals that are attached in such a way that they form a tube that appears to lack an outside opening. This characteristic has given the plant other common names, such as bottle gentian and blind gentian.

There is a legend that the gentian was named for Gentius, king of Illyria, an ancient country located on the Adriatic Sea, who is said to have used the plant medicinally. A Hungarian legend says that King Ladislas shot an arrow into the air, praying that the plant on which it landed could be used to fight the plague. The arrow landed on the gentian, and the

plague miraculously stopped.

Gentian roots contain a bitter chemical known as glucoside that has been used to purify the blood and ease stiff and aching backs. It has also been used as an antiseptic, to treat fevers, jaundice, dropsy, gout, pneumonia, epilepsy, and skin diseases. European settlers in America added it to gin or brandy to stimulate the appetite and aid in digestion. Some actually believed that glucoside could be used in a tonic to obtain eternal youth. The yellow gentian, *Gentiana lutea*, is the commercial source of gentian root and is used to flavor vermouth.

There are over 500 different gentians, mostly native to cool, wet places all over the world and all with the prettiest of blue-colored flowers, which blossom primarily in late summer and early fall. Those that are native to tundras and mountain-tops are often still in bloom when the first snows come; they finish their blooming cycle in the spring.

Gentians are difficult to grow in the garden, but they are so beautiful that any results will be worth the effort. Of all the gentians, the closed gentian is the easiest to grow. If the environmental conditions in which it grows in the wild can be matched, success will be greater. In nature, genetians are usually found in semishaded spots in wet meadows, at the edge of damp woods, or along the water.

Insects are attracted to gentians by the fragrant nectar found in their vaselike flowers, a substance so enticing that bees are forced to open the closed, bottle-shaped, deep blue flowers of bottle gentian, *Gentiana andrewsii*, and its relatives to reach the nectar and thereby pollinate the flowers. Because many flying insects avoid dark places, they would not likely enter the blue flowers of most gentians were it not for the translucent white patches found at the bottom of the petals. Species with light-colored flowers, such as *G. alba*, the yellow gentian, need no enticing markings.

The downy gentian, *G. puberulenta*, has deep blue flowers with five pointed petals that are clustered atop hairy stems and rough-edged leaves. The explorer's gentian, *G. calycosa*, has funnel-shaped blue to purple flowers with five rounded petals separated by fringed segments. The purple-tipped gentian, *G. algida*, has creamy white petals tipped with purple markings.

Prairie gentians are found in the genus *Eustoma*. Two are native to the warmer parts of North America and a third is found in the tropics of Central and South America. Sometimes called bluebells, they have cup-shaped flowers of pink, blue, or white. The most popular is lisianthus, *E. grandiflora,* a summer-blooming plant that has been popularized in the last decade as a cut flower.

MINT FAMILY

The bee balm, *Monarda didyma,* is a rapid-growing perennial that spreads its creeping roots to form large patches of brightly colored red or lavender summer flowers. Like catnip and sage, it is a member of the Mint Family, *Lamiaceae.* The genus *Monarda* was named for Nicholas Monardes, a sixteenth-century Spanish botanist and physician from Seville whose greatest interest was New World plants. The species name *didyma* is from a Greek word meaning "paired or twinned," and it refers to the two stamens found in each flower.

The bee balm, like all Mint Family members, is characterized by its square stem. It has a minty flavor useful in cooking and preserving and is sometimes called horsemint. Bee balm attracts hummingbirds and butterflies as well as bees. The tubular segments of the flowers make it difficult for many insects to pollinate them. It is thought that these plants were once used by Native Americans to relieve bee stings or other insect stings, thus its common name.

It was recorded by explorer John Bartram that the bee balm was used by the Native Americans that settled along the shores of Lake Ontario in what is now northern New York State, to make a mint-flavored tea known as Oswego tea. This tea became very popular in the colonies as a cure for upset stomachs and fever and was used as a substitute for the tea lost in the Boston Tea Party.

Wild bergamot, *M. fistulosa,* although not related to true bergamot, a member of the citrus family that is grown for its oil (the type used in lemon furniture polish), gets its name from the similarity of its scent to that of the fruit of true bergamot. Wild bergamot has lilac or pink blossoms and a penetrating meadowlike scent. The upper leaves are often stained with pale lilac tones that match the color of the flower bracts.

A lemon scent is also found in *M. citriodora,* commonly known as lemon mint. Native to the western part of North America, it has pink or white flowers with purple spots. Spotted horsemint, *M. punctata,* has yellow flowers with purple spots that are surrounded by leafy lilac bracts.

POPPY FAMILY

Many wildflowers are in the Poppy Family, *Papaveraceae;* some are in the true poppy genus, *Papaver.* What all Poppy Family members have in common is a tap root that reaches deep into the soil in search of water, making the plants very drought resistant.

The most common wildflower in the true poppy genus is *P. rhoeas,* commonly known as corn poppy or field poppy. This plant has bristly stems and bright orange-red flowers with black centers. Like most poppies, the leaves are finely dissected.

The corn poppy is the poppy of Flanders' Fields, well known as the plant that came into bloom on the grounds of the Flanders battlefield at the end of World War I. This poppy is often represented by the orange crêpe-paper flowers that are given out by veterans' organizations to commemorate those lost in war. The corn poppy is native to Europe and Asia, but it can now be found across North America.

The corn poppy makes an excellent vegetable. It contains no narcotic, as Oriental and opium poppies do, but it has been used medicinally. During the Middle Ages, corn-poppy juice was given to infants as a remedy for colic or sleeplessness, and dried petals were believed to calm hyperactive children. Pigments extracted from the petals were used as dye to color medicines and wine.

With golden-yellow petals as delicate as tissue paper, the California poppy, the state flower of California, adorns hillsides along the state's coast from late winter through late spring. In addition to bringing visual beauty to the landscape, California poppies fill the hills and dales with a delightful fragrance. These plants have lacy light-green leaves and, typical of the Poppy Family, the flowers have four petals and numerous stamens in the center. Spanish settlers called the California poppy *copa de oro*, or "cup of gold."

California poppies are botanically known as *Eschscholtzia californica*, for Johann Eschscholtz, a Russian professor of medicine who visited California with a plant-expedition team in 1815. Native Americans ate the leaves of the California poppy and used its roots as a pain-killer long before the plant was introduced into European gardens in the 1830's.

California poppy flowers close at night and on cloudy days and burst into color at the first hint of sunlight. This phenomenon is also characteristic of the Mexican poppy, *E. mexicana*, a smaller cousin of the California poppy, which has darker yellow flowers.

Plant breeders have bred the wild California poppy, developing garden strains that have single or double flowers ranging in color from cream-colored to yellow, to orange, to pink, to red. However, the simple, sprightly golden-yellow wildflower remains the favorite.

*O*ther examples of poppies are the white prickly poppy, *Argemone hispida*, and the red prickly poppy, *A. sanguinea*, whose stems and silver-colored lobed leaves are covered with sharp spines to protect the plant from straying animals. The generic name for prickly poppy is from the Greek word *argemon*, which means "cataract of the eye." It was once believed that plants in this genus cured eye disorders and cataracts. The leaves contain a deadly alkaloid, isoquinolin, but the stiff spines make it unlikely that these plants will be eaten. Prickly poppies are native to desert areas, where the least appealing plants are usually the most likely to survive; their flowers bloom throughout the summer.

The wind poppy, or flaming poppy, *Stylomecon heterophylla*, is the only species in its genus. Its flowers are a flaming red to orange color and bloom in the spring; its leaves are highly divided and contain a yellow sap. The wind poppy's seed capsule has an unusual shape: it looks like a ribbed toy top.

Hikers in the gorges and canyons of southern California and Arizona may see the spectacular Matilija poppy, *Romneya coulteri*, which stands shrublike—eight feet tall—and is covered in early summer with large, fragrant white flowers. Along seashores, the yellow-horned poppy, *Glaucium flavum*, provides blooms of bright yellow over blue-green leaves. Its common name derives from the sickle shape of its seed pod.

PRIMROSE FAMILY

The Primrose Family, *Primulaceae*, is most at home in the Northern Temperate Zone. The various wild shooting stars are among this family's best-known members. They are cousins to the garden ornamentals primula, primrose, and cyclamen.

Native from southern Alaska across to the midwestern United States and south into Mexico, shooting star, *Dodocatheon pulchellum*, blooms in late spring or early summer, depending on the climate. Its small flowers bloom on leafless stems with petals swept back like trailing flames. *D. meadia*, known as the eastern shooting star, is a similar species found in the eastern half of North America. The foliage of both plants grows in a ground-hugging rosette and disappears after the plants have bloomed.

Legend has it that wherever a star falls to earth, these wildflowers will appear. The generic name *Dodocatheon* was formed from Greek words meaning "flower of the twelve gods." When the early settlers in America first moved west and found shooting stars growing abundantly in open fields, they called them prairie flowers. American cowslip is another common name.

Shooting stars are the most versatile of plants, thriving in sunny meadows or shady woods. They are drought tolerant when established, but as a self-protective measure, they may not bloom if there is insufficient moisture. They have the ability to self-pollinate, so they can survive even where insects are scarce.

The western shooting star, or Padre's shooting star, *D. clevlandii*, has mostly pink flowers with white and yellow bands at the base of the petals. A slow grower with a flowering stem, it fills meadows and open woodlands with color in early spring. The species was named for San Diego botanist Daniel Cleveland.

GERANIUM FAMILY

The garden geranium, *Pelargonium*, a plant that children traditionally give on Mother's Day, is actually a close relative of *Geranium*, a wildflower very different in appearance. Both, however, are members of the Geranium Family, *Geraniaceae*.

It was the wild geranium plant that scientists first used to study the interaction between the insect world and the plant world. The wild geranium cannot self-pollinate, because the male and female parts of the flower mature at different times. It is therefore pollinated only by insects, usually the honeybee.

Geranium is the Greek word for "crane." The flower's common name, crane's bill or stork's bill, refers to the shape of the seed pod, which looks like a bird's beak. When the seed pod matures, it bursts open with surprising suddenness and shoots the seeds great distances.

Legend has it that the wild geranium descended from the mallow flower. It is said that the prophet Mohammed once washed a shirt in a stream and laid it on a mallow bed to dry; the flowers blushed deep pink at the honor of holding Mohammed's clothes and were given the name *geranium*.

Wild geraniums were treasured for their medicinal value. Tea made from the boiled roots was used to treat sore throats and mouth ulcers, and tea made from the leaves was used to treat dysentery. Native Americans used wild geranium as an astringent and as a tonic, and the powdered root was used to treat cuts, because it contains a high amount of tannin, which helps stop bleeding.

There are over 300 different species of wild geraniums sharing a number of characteristics. The flowers have five petals, which may be white, red, pink, purple, or blue and usually bloom in very loose clusters during the summer. The leaves are often hairy, sometimes lobed, and sometimes deeply cut and divided.

One of the best known of the wild geraniums is *G. sanguineum prostratum*, sometimes called *G. lancastrense*. The veined flowers are reddish purple or rose pink and they bloom above round lobed leaves. Dove's foot crane's bill, *G. molle*, has kidney-shaped to round, lobed leaves and bright rose-pink flowers with notched petals. *G. maculatum*, commonly called wild crane's bill, spotted crane's bill, or alumroot, has deeply indented five-lobed spotted leaves that look like maple leaves and rose-lavender flowers. Occasionally the stamens are a delicate shade of blue.

Herb gardens often include the geranium Herb Robert, *G. robertianum*. Its bristly stems are red, which gives the plant another common name, red robin; the divided leaves resemble the leaves of a fern. Some find the scent of the plant disagreeable, while others find it refreshing and reminiscent of the countryside. Herb Robert's flowers are bright pink and have wedge-shaped petals.

Another Geranium Family plant with the name stork's bill is in the *Erodium* genus. It is very similar to the *Geranium* genus's stork's bill, with finely divided leaves, five-petaled flowers, and pointed seed pods that resemble a stork's beak; sometimes it is called heron's bill. Plants in this genus include *E. chamaedryoides*, a plant with rose-veined white flowers. Known as alpine geranium, it is actually native to the Mediterranean islands of Corsica, Minorca, and Majorca. *E. cicutarium*, an annual plant used for forage, has pink or purple flowers. It is commonly known as alfilaria, red-stemmed filaree, wild musk, pin clover, or pin grass.

PHLOX FAMILY

The Phlox Family, *Polemoniaceae*, is a small family of annuals and perennials. Of the 18 genera in the family, *Phlox*, *Linanthus*, and *Polemonium* are the most common.

With the exception of one species that is native to Siberia, the *Phlox* genus is native to North America. It was one of the first plants taken from the New World to Europe by early explorers. The Europeans regarded phlox highly and bred many garden varieties from it before reintroducing it to North America. The phlox symbolized a proposal of love and a hope for sweet dreams. The genus name comes from the similar Greek word for "flame," as bright reddish pink is a common color among phlox.

Sweetly scented, especially at dusk, the phlox, like many wildflowers, has been valued for its medicinal qualities. Crushed leaves were mixed with water and used for upset stomachs, sore eyes, and skin diseases, and an extract made from the leaves was used as a laxative.

Most low-growing phlox are spring blooming. The wild blue phlox, also called wild sweet William, *P. divaricata*, has lance-shaped leaves and light blue flowers that bloom in loose clusters atop single stems. Plants from the eastern part of North America have a notch in each of the four petals, while those from western North America do not. Botanists describe the flower form of all phlox as salverform, which means "tray-shaped," because of the flat surface formed by the five petals at the point at which they flare from a short tube.

Found in alpine meadows and on rocky slopes, the mountain phlox, *P. diffusa*, has pale white to lilac flowers that bloom in late spring and early summer on mound-forming plants with needlelike leaves.

Creeping phlox, *P. stolonifera*, has violet to purple flowers with oval petals and creeping stems with oval leaves. Unlike many other phlox, it grows best in moist, shaded conditions. It is similar in growth habit, but not in appearance or environmental needs, to moss pink, *P. subulata*. Also known as mountain pink, moss pink has close-set, linear, almost needlelike leaves. Its flowers may be pink, white, magenta, or blue. Moss pink grows best in dry sunny fields; in the garden, it fills spaces between crevices in walkways and stone walls.

Most phlox are perennial, but there is also an annual member of the genus, *P. drummondi*, which originated in south-central Texas. The flowers of this species are red and showy and are borne on short stems. Many garden varieties in mixed colors have been developed from this wildflower. It blooms all summer and does especially well where nights are cool and there is an abundance of moisture. Annual phlox, as it is known, was named for Thomas Drummond, a nineteenth-century, Scottish botanist who sent seeds of the plant to England in 1835 after a plant-exploration trip to Texas.

*T*he mountain, or California, phlox is in another related genus, *Linanthus*. The large-flowered linanthus, *L. grandiflorus*, is a spring-blooming annual that has dense clusters of silky white flowers tinged with pink or lavender. These plants usually dry out and disappear in the wild during the summer dry season, but they can be kept growing in cultivated gardens if they are watered.

*T*he *Polemonium* genus was named for the early Greek philosopher Polemon. Jacob's ladder, *P. caeruleum*, was named for the runglike arrangement of the leaves on its stem that make it look like ladder. The plant was named for Jacob and his dream of angels ascending a ladder into heaven. The violet bell-shaped blooms nod when they are buds but straighten out as they open.

IRIS FAMILY

The Iris Family, *Iridaceae*, contains about 60 genera of perennials that grow from bulbs, corms, or rhizomes. The family includes many ornamentals, cultivated and wild; yields some medicinal products; and includes some plants with minor economic uses.

Although irises are cultivated in many formal perennial gardens, there are also a large number in the wild. The name *iris* is derived from the Greek word for "rainbow," because the flowers bloom in so many colors. One of the duties of Iris, the goddess of the rainbow, was to lead the souls of women who had died to the Elysian Fields, and so the ancient Greeks planted irises on the graves of their loved ones to ensure this. Another of her duties was to bring peace after a confrontation between the gods, just as the rainbow signals the end of a storm. The word *iris* also translated as "eye of heaven," a name given both to the rainbow and to the center of the eye.

Because of the way the petals flutter in the wind, irises are often called flags. They have been regarded in Japan as a symbol of masculinity and are the basis of the *fleur-de-lis*, the French symbol of royalty and heraldry. As long ago as the first century A.D., the French used the iris to symbolize their victories. Clovis I, the Frankish king from 481 to 511 A.D., was the first king to adopt the iris as a symbol of victory. This symbol was revived by Louis VII, when it was first called *fleur-de-lis*, "flower of Louis." Charles IV, who reigned from 1322 to 1328, was the first king to include the iris on the French banner. The iris is also the state flower of Tennessee.

Iris roots were once used medicinally by Native Americans to treat skin sores and as a diuretic and cathartic, but their use is no longer recommended, as they can be harmful if ingested in large quantities, causing shortness of breath and intestinal inflammation.

The iris flower is a unique one, composed of six petals: three erect petals known as standards and three drooping petals that are called falls. The leaves are long, stiff, narrow, and sword-shaped.

One of the smallest irises, the dwarf crested iris, *I. cristata*, grows only four to eight inches tall in woodlands and along streams. Its flowers are blue to purple and have a yellow crest on their falls. One of the best-suited irises for lakeshores, marshes, and swamps is the yellow flag, *I. pseudoacorus*, a European native now growing wild across North America. Its flowers are yellow and have dark lines on their broad falls. Swamps and marshes are also home to the blue flag, *I. versicolor*, whose veined blue or purple flowers bloom in early summer. It is the veins on these flowers that guide insects to the nectar; and while they are making the trip, pollination takes place.

Other common irises are the dwarf blue flag, *I. verna*, with purple flowers that have yellow blotches on the falls; the southern blue flag, *I. virginica*, with a similar-looking but larger flower; the Rocky Mountain iris, *I. missouriensis*, with yellow, white, and purple markings on blue to lilac falls; and the red flag, *I. fulva*, with reddish brown to bronze flowers. The Oregon blue flag or tough leaf iris, *I. tenax*, has narrow but strong leaves that the Native Americans used for making cord and rope. The species name is derived from the Latin word for "tenacious." Douglas's iris, *I. douglasiana*, produces copious amounts of nectar and therefore attracts large numbers of insects. A tender species native to the coastal areas of western North America, it has tan, blue, or reddish purple flowers that bloom in early spring on one- to two-foot stems.

MADDER FAMILY

Bluets, *Hedyotis caerulea*, formerly called *Houstonia caerulea*, are members of the Madder Family, *Rubiaceae*, as are madder (a dye), quinine, coffee, and gardenias. Bluets are one of the few nontropical members of the family. They are low-growing plants, only four or so inches tall, with four-petaled, yellow-centered pale blue flowers that grow in large patches and bloom in midspring atop a fine tangle of narrow foliage. They're as delicate as fine enamel and are delightful to watch swaying in the breeze. Wherever bluets are found, bees and butterflies, especially the clouded sulfur and the painted lady butterflies, will be nearby.

The genus *Houstonia* was named for William Houston, an eighteenth-century Scottish surgeon, botanist, and writer, who was a friend of Linnaeus. The name was given as a token of friendship; Houston really had nothing to do with discovering or popularizing the flower. It was only recently that the genus name was changed to *Hedyotis*. Another species of bluet, *H. lanceolata*, is taller with clusters of white to pale purple flowers and blooms somewhat later in the spring.

Other common names for the bluet include innocence, for its pastel coloration; eyebright, for the bright yellow center of the flower; Venus's pride; and little washerwoman. Bluets are also called Quaker ladies, because the flowers are similar in shape to the little white hats that Quaker women once wore. Native to Canada and the eastern half of the United States, bluets are annual wildflowers. Their seeds germinate in fall and the plants live throughout the winter and bloom in the spring before dropping seeds to start the cycle again.

FLAX FAMILY

The Flax Family, *Linaceae*, contains about 14 genera of annuals and perennials. Of these, flax, in the *Linum* genus, is the most common.

Flax has been known since earliest recorded history as the source of linen. Because of this, it is one of the most economically valuable plants and one that has served civilization as, primarily, a nonfood plant longer than any other: prehistoric lake dwellers in Switzerland made fishnet and rope from its stems and ate its oily seeds; the Egyptians used linen to wrap mummies; the Chinese used the cloth for noblemen's clothing; and Native Americans used *Linum virginianum*, which unlike most flax has yellow flowers, for many of the same purposes. American colonists did not cultivate flax widely at first, because of the popularity of cotton.

The flax of commerce today is *L. usitatissimum*, an

annual grown for the fiber of the stem from which flax fiber and linen are derived and for the seeds, from which linseed oil and linseed cake and meal are derived. Flax is raised in North America in Minnesota, North and South Dakota, and Canada.

Linseed oil, the basis of paints, varnishes, printing ink, and linoleum, is derived from flax seeds. Linseed is also used to smooth the skin, in poultices, as a sedative, in cough syrups, and in the treatment of genito-urinary tract diseases. The genus name, *Linum*, is the basis for other familiar words, such as *line, lingerie, linament, lint,* and, of course, *linen.*

Wild blue flax, *Linum perenne,* has deep blue flowers and grows to a height of two feet. Prairie flax, *L. lewisii,* also has blue blooms that arch to one side of its slender stems. The flowers are open only in the morning, so they do not make good cut flowers, although they are often pressed.

WATER LILY FAMILY

The water lilies in the *Nymphaea* genus are not members of the Lily Family and are not even related to it—they are members of the Water Lily Family, *Nymphaeaceae.* The genus and family name comes from the mythological nymphs who lived in secluded ponds and lakes in ancient Greece. The family contains eight genera of aquatic plants, the most popular of which are the water lily and lotus. All are ornamental, and some lotuses have edible seeds and rhizomes.

Water lilies, including the sacred lotus, have shiny leaves that float on the water and showy flowers that are held above the still waters of shallow lakes and ponds. Many cultures have regarded the water lily as a symbol of perfection, beauty, and purity, because the flowers are held high above the muddy waters in which the roots grow.

Different species of water lilies bloom at different times during the day. The white water lily, *N. odorata,* has snowy white fragrant flowers that bloom from summer until the first frost, but the flowers open only in the morning. The small white water lily, *N. tetragona,* has smaller flowers that open only in the afternoon.

After a water lily blooms, it forms seeds, which float on the water until they become waterlogged. They will then fall to the lake or pond bed, where they germinate and sprout into new plants. The overripe seed capsule of the yellow water lily, *N. lutea,* smells of alcohol; this has given it the common name brandy bottle.

The young, unopened leaves of the water lily are said to enhance the flavor of soups and stews. They were thought to act as strong anti-aphrodisiacs and to cure insomnia and were used as an antiseptic and an astringent. The leaves were also used in lotions to soften the skin.

The American lotus, *Nelumbo lutea,* has leaves that can grow to two feet across that serve as a sunning spot for frogs and a landing strip for dragonflies. Beautiful white flowers bloom above the water, and as the petals fall, the golden center turns into a cone-shaped seed pod as decorative as the flowers. Native Americans treasured the tubers, which taste like sweet potatoes when baked. In days gone by, people also boiled and roasted the immature seeds, which have the flavor of chestnuts.

*T*hroughout the ages, people have sent bouquets of wildflowers to others to express certain messages. It is as though these flowers have a language of their own.
The following wildflowers and what they symbolize first appeared in a book called *Language of Flowers,* published by Kate Greenaway in 1884. They represent the Victorian tradition of using flowers and plants to express both positive and negative feelings.

Bellflower	*Constancy, gratitude*	Geranium	*Constancy, availability*
Buttercup	*Ingratitude, childishness*	Goldenrod	*Encouragement, precaution*
Butterfly weed	*Let go*	Harebell	*Submission, grief*
Canterbury bells	*Acknowledgment*	Iris	*Thinking of you, message*
Cardinal flower	*Distinction*	White lily	*Purity, sweetness*
Celandine	*Joys to come*	Yellow lily	*Falsehood, gaiety*
Chicory	*Frugality*	Lobelia	*Malevolence*
Four-leaf clover	*Good luck, be mine*	Lotus	*Eloquence*
Purple clover	*Provident*	Lotus flower	*Estranged love*
Red clover	*Industry*	Lotus leaf	*Recantation*
White clover	*Think of me*	Lupine	*Voraciousness, imagination*
Columbine	*Folly*	Mint	*Virtue*
Purple columbine	*Resolved to win*	Pasque flower	*No claims*
Red columbine	*Anxious and trembling*	Penstemon	*Pleasure*
Coreopsis	*Always cheerful*	Phlox	*Unanimity*

Cowslip	*Pensiveness, winning grace*	Ranunculus	*Radiant with charms*
Cyclamen	*Diffidence*	Wild Ranunculus	*Ingratitude*
Daisy	*Innocence*	Rudbeckia	*Justice*
Garden daisy	*Share of sentiments*	Shamrock	*Lightheartedness*
Michelmas daisy	*Afterthought, remembrance*	Dwarf sunflower	*Adoration*
Ox-eye daisy	*Patience*	Tail sunflower	*Haughtiness*
Wild daisy	*I will think of it*	Common thistle	*Austerity*
White daisy	*Innocence*	Scottish thistle	*Retaliation*
Dandelion	*Oracle, faithfulness*	Trillium	*Modest beauty*
Daylily	*Coquetry*	Blue violet	*Faithfulness*
Eupatorium	*Delay*	Sweet violet	*Modesty*
Evening primrose	*Inconstancy*	Yellow violet	*Rural happiness*
Flax	*Domestic industry, fate, kindness felt*	Water lily	*Purity of heart*
Dried flax	*Utility*	Windflower	*Forsaken*
Fleur-de-lis	*Flame*	Yarrow	*War*

A native of coastal Alaska, the arctic daisy, *Chrysanthemum arcticum,* grows close to the ground to prevent damage by rigorous northern elements.

Similar in appearance to the arctic daisy is the Shasta daisy, *Chrysanthemum maximum,* a naturally occurring hybrid of two other wild daisies; it fills summer gardens, fields, and roadsides with glistening white blooms.

Left: Erigeron glaucous is commonly known as beach aster or seaside daisy and grows wild along the coast from southern California to northern Oregon.

The flowers of autumn sneeze-weed, *Helenium autumnale,* do not really cause sneezing because their pollen is much heavier than the air and quickly sinks to the ground.

The pretty flowers of painted daisy, *Chrysanthemum coccineum,* are dried and used to produce the insecticide pyrethrum.

The white markings at the ends of the petals of the members of the *Layia* genus have given this group of flowers its common name— tidy tips.

The *Rudbeckia* genus was named for Swedish botanist, Olaf Rudbeck, who is considered the father of modern botany. Flowers from any species in this genus can be used to make an excellent gold-colored dye.

The black-eyed Susan, *Rudbeckia hirta*, is native to the Appalachian highlands, although it has spread to all regions of the United States.

The annual calliopsis, *Coreopsis tinctoria*, is sometimes known as tickseed because its seeds resemble ticks. At one time it was believed that the seeds repelled insects, although that was later found to be untrue.

Preceding pages: A lone arrowhead plant in the genus *Sagittaria* stands out against a profuse bloom of perennial tickseed.

The high, centered blooms of *Ratibida columnaris* so closely resemble a sombrero that the flower has been given the common name of Mexican hat.

The genus name *Echinacea* derives from the Greek word *echinos,* which means "hedge-hog," and refers to the bristles found along the leaves and stems of the plant.

The purple coneflower, *Echinacea purpurea,* is a stiff, coarse plant with beautiful, long-lasting flowers.

Encelia californica, bush sunflower, is native to southern California and the Baja Peninsula and grows into a large, bushy plant five feet or taller.

Gaillardia pulchella, native to
the southwestern United States,
is commonly known as Indian
blanket because the colors of
the flowers are the same as those
used by the Native Americans
of that region in making
blankets.

Preceding pages: Indian blanket has another common name, firewheel, given for the circular patterns on the flowers, which emulate the colors of a fire.

The tall and mighty common sunflower, *Helianthus annuus,* is the state flower of Kansas. The sunflower is grown commercially for both its seeds and its oil.

Although some consider the dandelion, *Taraxacum officinale*, to be a vicious weed, others cultivate it for use in salads and wine.

What child hasn't delighted in blowing on the seed heads of a dandelion and watching the fluffy specks float away in the breeze?

The fluffy flowers in the *Eupatorium* genus are sometimes known as hardy ageratum because they so closely resemble that annual flower.

Chicory, *Cichorium intybus*, is a common roadside wildflower cultivated for use in salads and coffee. The flowers open in the morning but close up by early afternoon.

Spotted Joe Pye weed, *Eupatorium maculatum*, was used by Native Americans to treat a number of ailments, including typhoid fever, and it was considered good luck for men to chew it before they went courting.

Eupatorium perfoliatum
is commonly known as
thoroughwort or boneset
because it was believed at one
time that sprinkling it on the
skin around a broken bone
would help the bone to heal.

Like most asters, New England aster, *Aster
novae-angliae,* has a radiating flower that is
named for the Greek word for "star," *aster.*

Aster linariifolius is commonly known as sandpaper aster and is one of the more than 75 species of aster native to the United States.

The ancient Greeks believed
that asters were made from
stardust.

Flowers of the New England aster are beautifully variable, ranging from lavender to blue to white.

Leafy aster, *Aster foliaceus,* grows in moist woods on roadsides and in mountain meadows.

Although most members
of the *Solidago* genus are
known as goldenrods, *S.
bicolor* is called silverrod or
white goldenrod because the
flowers are silvery white.

Solidago caesia is commonly
known as either blue-stemmed
goldenrod because the color
of the stems is blue to purple,
or wreath goldenrod, because
of its use in decorations.

Seaside goldenrod, *Solidago
sempervirens*, fills sand
dunes from Newfoundland
to coastal Virginia with
mounds of fall gold color.

Closely related to the prairie blazing star is the dense blazing star, or spiked gayfeather, *Liatris spicata,* which adds rich color to autumn gardens and roadsides, especially where the soil is moist.

Prairie blazing star, *Liatris pycnostachya,* is one of the few members of the daisy family whose flowers appear in a spike. Unlike other flowers, the blooms open from the top downwards.

The woolly daisy, *Eriophyllum wallacei,* is an annual wildflower that thrives in sandy desert soil.

Native to Europe, common yarrow, *Achillea millefolium,* is often planted in places where soil erosion control is needed, as the roots form thick mats that hold the soil in place.

The genus name for yarrow, *Achillea,* comes from Achilles, who was said to have carried the plant in battle to treat wounded soldiers; yarrow really does contain chemicals that help blood clot more quickly.

Despite its unpopularity, bull thistle, *Cirsium volgare*, is a common pasture plant (hence its name) that produces fine honey.

Although the sale of Canada thistle, *Cirsium arvense*, is illegal in 37 U.S. states because of its aggressive growth, the fast-creeping roots and tufted airborne seeds of already established plants still allow it to flourish.

Spiny-leaved sow thistle, *Sonchus asper*, is an Old World native whose leaves were once used as a potherb.

A Rocky Mountain wild-
flower garden comes to life
with Indian paintbrush,
Castilleja coccinea, a plant
that Native Americans used
to soothe burned skin and
cure the burning sting of a
centipede.

The colorful bracts surrounding the flowers of the Indian paintbrush give it its beauty; the actual flowers are small, yellowish-green, and insignificant.

Following pages:
Davidson's penstemon,
Penstemon davidsonii,
thrives in the cool, rainy
climate of the region from
British Columbia to
Oregon. Other penstemons
prefer hot, desertlike
conditions.

A Native American legend
about the Indian paintbrush
tells of a brave who was trying
to paint a sunset and, having
difficulty, asked the Great
Spirit for help. He was pre-
sented with paintbrushes
dripping in bright colors,
which, when placed on the
ground after the painting was
finished, turned into flowers.

The deserts of California and Arizona are home to *Penstemon pseudospectabilis*, one of 250 species of penstemons; all but two of the species are native to North America.

Rocky Mountain penstemon, *Penstemon strictus*, like other members of the genus, is known as beardtongue because of its prominent stamen covered with a fuzzy growth of hair.

Linaria vulgaris is called butter-and-eggs for the coloration of its flowers. It is a European native that has become established in many areas of the United States.

Growing as tall as eight feet, common mullein, *Verbascum thapsus,* is often called Jacob's staff and shepherd's club. Another characteristic—fuzzy leaves—has earned the plant still more names, like velvet plant and flannel leaf.

Like other members of the *Linaria* genus, old field toad-flax, *Linaria canadensis,* is sometimes called spurred snapdragon because of the shape of its flower.

Linaria maroccana, an annual toadflax species native to Morocco, is found across the United States today. The flower's spot attracts hummingbirds and long-tongued insects to the nectar deep in the base of the flower.

Lily Family

Southern red lily, *Lilium catesbaei,* is also called pine lily because it is native to the bogs and wet pinelands of the southeastern United States.

Following pages: Sometimes called glacier lily, the avalanche lily is related to the true lily, although it is botanically known as *Erythronium grandiflorum.* As its common names suggest, it is found in mountain meadows, along streambanks, and in the woods near melting snow.

Lilium superbum is one of a number of lilies known as turk's cap lilies because the upswept petals of the flower give it the shape of a turban.

According to a Korean legend, the tiger lily, *Lilium tigrinum*, came into being when a tiger was transformed into a flower, which spread rapidly in search of its caretaker.

Trout lily, *Erythronium americanum*, was named because it blooms during trout season, and because its spotted leaves coincidentally resemble the markings on a trout. The corm from which it grows is shaped like a dog's tooth, also giving it the name dogtooth violet.

The flowers of the Washington lily, *Lilium washingtonianum*, are white but fade to pink as they age; during midsummer, they cover the mountains of Washington and Oregon with color.

The sego lily, *Calochortus nutallii*, is the state flower of Utah and was a staple food that kept the Mormons from starving when they first settled in that region.

Deserts and dry slopes are the home of the desert mariposa, *Calochortus kennedyi*, which has yellow to vermilion flowers during the late spring.

The markings on the flowers
of some members of the
Calochortus genus, including
C. superbus, give them the
common name of mariposa
lily; *mariposa* is the Spanish
word for "butterfly."

Everything comes in threes with trillium, including the name, which is from the Latin for three: the plant has three petals, three sepals, and three leaves.

Trillium grandiflorum, the largest-flowering trillium, is sometimes called wake robin because it blooms in early spring.

Buttercup Family

It is said that if a buttercup is held beneath one's chin and produces a rich golden color on the skin, the holder likes butter.

The buttercup, in the *Ranunculus* genus, is sometimes called crowfoot because of the shape of the leaf; just about all buttercups have waxy yellow flowers that greet the first warm weather of spring.

Elk and moose make a
regular diet of elkslip, *Caltha
leptosepala*, a close relative
of the buttercup with white
flowers instead of the more
common yellow.

A relative of both buttercup and elkslip is
marsh marigold, *Caltha palustris*, whose
perky flowers and glistening leaves color
springtime wetlands throughout North
America.

Each of the five petals of wild columbine, *Aquilegia canadensis*, stretches back into a long spur, which hides nectar deep inside from bees, long-tongued moths, and hummingbirds.

The state flower of Colorado is the blue columbine *Aquileqia caerulea.* Its names come from the columbine's resemblance to a bird: columbine means dove and *Aquileqia* is Latin for "eagle."

Some species of anemone, like *Anemone parviflora*, have flowers borne on short hairy stalks; after the blooms are pollinated by crawling insects, the stems stretch upward so the seeds can be blown by the wind.

The wood anemone, *Anemone quinquefolia*, as its species name suggests, has leaves divided into five parts; it blooms by the thousands on the slopes of the Rocky Mountains in early spring.

Anemone pulsatilla is commonly known as Pasqueflower because it blooms in the spring during the Pasque season of Passover and Easter.

Western anemone, *Anemone occidentalis,* is sometimes called Old Man of the Mountain because of the appearance of the long-haired seed heads.

Western anemone is easy to recognize in any season by its finely divided, lacy leaves, hairy stems, and showy, creamy flowers with golden centers.

Rue anemone, *Anemonella thalictroides,* gets its common name because its foliage happens to look like rue and its flowers look like those of the anemone.

Preceding pages: The hair-clad lavender flowers of Pasqueflower open on silky stems before the deeply lobed, lacy leaves appear. Both the roots and the leaves contain an alkaloid substance poisonous to livestock.

Because of the compact, thimble-shaped seed head of *Anemone virginiana,* it (and other anemone species) is commonly called thimbleweed.

Queen Anne, who loved to make lace, gave her name to Queen Anne's lace, *Daucus carota*, a lacy wildflower that is closely related to the garden carrot.

Pea Family

The clover has figured into many legends as a symbol of fertility, domestic virtue, and good luck.

The leaf of the clover has been used by Christians as a symbol of the Trinity and has lent its name to complex intersections on modern highways.

Hop, or yellow, clover, *Trifolium agrarium*, is usually found in open fields, from which its species name is derived. As the flowers wither and die, they fold downward and resemble dried hops, hence one of the plant's common names.

White, or Dutch clover, *Trifolium repens* is one of the most important fodder plants and is often sown in pastures. It is also an important plant in crop rotation schemes, as it, like other legumes, fixes nitrogen into the soil, therefore enriching it.

The state flower of Vermont, red clover, *Trifolium pratense*, has the typical sweet scent so commonly associated with a meadow. In addition to making good honey, the dried flower heads make a delicious tea.

Like all clovers, the roots,
stems, leaves, and flowers of
desert clover, *Trifolium macro-
cephalum,* are edible, but they
are more palatable if slightly
cooked or soaked in salt water.

Prairie clover, *Petalostemon ornatum,* has
a deep tap root which allows it to survive
droughts. At one time, the roots were used to
make a tea that reduced fever, especially fever
associated with measles.

Along the highways of the southwestern United States, crimson clover, *Trifolium incarnatum*, is a favorite. Like most other clovers, it is a native of Europe, introduced to the United States for forage and crop rotation.

The white false indigo, *Baptisia leucantha,* is native to the southern United States. The genus name comes from the Greek *baptizein,* which means "to dye," because the plant's pigment was once used as a substitute for true indigo dye.

Blue false indigo, *Baptisia australis,* is not from Australia as its species name might indicate; it is from the southern United States.

The Texas bluebonnet, *Lupinus texensis,* grows along roadways throughout Texas.

The genus name for the lupine, *Lupinus,* is derived from the Latin *lupus,* which means "wolf," because it was once believed that these plants robbed nutrients from the soil, the way that a wolf robs the shepherd.

The blue lupine, *Lupinus perennis,* is the most common lupine in the eastern United States. Most other species are found in the southwest and along the Pacific coast.

Bluebell Family

There are two theories surrounding the derivation of the common name of *Campanula rotundifolia*, the American harebell: one is that the plant is found in fields where hares live; another, more mysterious, theory is that witches used this plant to turn themselves into hares.

Piper's bluebell, *Campanula piperi*, is native to the Olympic Mountains in Washington state and, growing only four inches tall, is a perfect plant for a rock garden.

Tall bellflower, *Campanula americana*, can grow as tall as seven feet. It has flat, star-shaped flowers instead of the bell-shaped flowers of its cousins.

One of the best plants for attracting hummingbirds into a late summer and early fall garden is the cardinal flower, *Lobelia cardinalis*. The flowers are too long and slim to be pollinated by most insects.

The lobelia genus was named for Matthew de l'Obel, physician to King James I. For many years great lobelia, *Lobelia siphilitica*, was believed to be a remedy for syphilis.

Violet Family

Although called Canada violet, *Viola canadensis* is found throughout most of the United States in addition to Canada. It is one of the tallest violets, reaching heights of up to 18 inches.

Common blue violet, *Viola papilionacea*, wears many hats. It is the state flower of Illinois, Rhode Island, New Jersey, and Wisconsin; it is the flower of March; and was the emblem of the French Bonapartists.

Violet flowers are edible and are a lovely garnish on cold soups and salads. The flowers, leaves, and seeds have also been used for a number of medicinal purposes throughout the ages.

The mountains of western North America and northeastern Asia are home to the yellow-flowered stream violet, *Viola glabella.*

Viola tricolor is commonly known as Johnny jump-up because of its bright and cheery flowers. A Greek legend says the flower was once pure white until struck by one of Cupid's arrows.

Milkweed Family

The rich deep scent of milkweed, *Asclepias syriaca*, fills the air wherever it grows. Young shoots can be cooked and eaten like asparagus.

Milkweed is one of the most fragrant wildflowers; as appealing as its aroma are the silky parachutes released in the fall from its seed pods.

Milkweeds can be very tall and will climb and entwine themselves around other plants like this cholla cactus.

Butterfly weed, *Asclepias tuberosa*, is one of the few milkweeds without a milky sap. Its bright orange flowers are very attractive to butterflies, especially the monarch butterfly.

While most milkweeds are found wild in sandy fields, prairies, dry plains, scrublands, and deserts, the swamp milkweed, *Asclepias incarnata*, is, as its common name indicates, native to marshes and wet meadows.

The state flower of Montana, *Lewisia rediviva*, is commonly known as bitterroot for the starchy, edible root that was a staple of the Native Americans. The bitterness, which lies in the husk, disappears after boiling.

Siskiyou Lewisia, *Lewisia cotyledon,* is another member of the genus that was named for Captain Meriwether Lewis who first collected it when he explored the western United States with Clark in the early 1800's.

Evening Primrose Family

There are two types of plants in the *Oenothera genus*. One blooms during the day and is usually called sundrop. The other is night-blooming and is usually called evening primrose. Showy evening primrose, *Oenothera speciosa*, defies the naming system by blooming during the day.

Wine cup clarkia, *Clarkia purpurea*, got its common name from its burgundy-colored flower petals. The genus was named for William Clark who, with Meriwether Lewis, first crossed the Rocky Mountains in 1806.

Native to California, *Clarkia concinna*, is commonly known as red ribbons (although its petals are bright pink) because the petals are so finely cut.

Clarkia amoena, farewell to spring, blooms intermixed with prairie grass in late spring. It was given its common name because it is one of the last flowers to bloom before spring turns to summer.

The most common evening primrose is *Oenothera biennis.* Evening primroses generally have nothing in common with true primroses, except for some species that have flowers that smell similar.

Showy evening primrose and other members of the *Oenothera* genus were introduced to Europe from the New World as early as 1600. The genus name means "wine imbibing," and was given to the plant for its supposed ability to increase one's desire for wine.

The white blooms of *Oenothera albicaulis*, prairie evening primrose, take on a pink tinge as they begin to fade, but not before they have brightened the slopes of the Rocky Mountains and their adjoining plains.

Oenothera pallida, white, or desert evening primrose, is found in deserts and along the Pacific coast, where it is tolerant of salt spray and has strong roots that bind sand dunes.

The bloom of *Oenothera caespitosa*, gumbo lily, is closed for the morning, but when it opens, it will reveal heart-shaped petals and a flower four inches across.

The bottle gentian, *Gentiana andrewsii* (left), is very similar in color to the explorer's gentian, *Gentiana calycosa* (right), but its cylindrical flowers remain nearly closed at the tips.

Named for an Illyrian king, Gentius, who first discovered the medicinal properties of its root, the gentian has been used to relieve backaches, fever, intestinal gas, jaundice, gout, and skin disease.

Mint Family

Bee balm, *Monarda didyma*, is attractive to bees, butterflies, and especially hummingbirds, which are attracted to the red flowers. It is also known as Oswego tea because the Oswego Indians who settled along Lake Ontario used the leaves to make tea.

Known as dotted mint or
horsemint, *Monarda punctata*
has the spotted flowers that its
name suggests.

Like all members of the genus
Monarda, lemon mint, *Monarda
citriodora*, has square stems. It
earned its common name from
the lemony fragrance of the
leaves.

Poppy Family

Preceding pages: Wild bergamot, *Monarda fistulosa,* has shaggy blossoms with a penetrating meadow fragrance. Its common name comes from the similarity of its fragrance and fruit to those of the bergamot orange tree.

Mexican gold, *Eschscholtzia mexicana,* is a petite relative of the California poppy; both are native to southern California and northern Mexico.

Following pages: The California poppy genus was named for Johann F. von Eschscholtz, a professor of medicine who visited California with a Russian expedition in 1915.

Native Americans ate the foliage of the California poppy, *Eschscholtzia californica,* and used its roots as a painkiller.

The Iceland poppy, *Papaver nudicaule*, is native to the Arctic regions of North America, Asia, and Europe. Like all poppies, it has fine petals that have the appearance of crepe paper.

White prickly poppy, *Argemone albiflora*, withstands desert heat and drought. The genus name comes from the Greek for "cataract of the eye," as some species were once believed to cure eye disorders.

Growing shrublike up to eight feet tall from the Grand Canyon to California's mountains, the Matilija poppy, *Romneya coulteri*, has crinkled petals and a delightful fragrance.

Primrose Family

A legend says that wherever a star falls to earth, the shooting star, *Dodocatheon*, appears. The plant is well named, as its swept-back petals give it the appearance of a shooting star.

Following pages: When early settlers first moved west, they found large numbers of shooting stars growing in prairies, and therefore called them "prairie pointers."

The shape of the flowers has given shooting star a second common name, birdbill. The genus name is from the Greek for "flower of the twelve gods."

Geranium Family

Sticky geranium, *Geranium viscosissimum*, is typically a northwestern wildflower that flourishes in woods, meadows, and on mountains.

There are nearly 800 wild species in the genus *Geranium*. *Geranium erianthum*, is native to western Canada, Alaska, and eastern Asia.

Herb Robert, *Geranium robertianum*, has a strong odor which some find unpleasant, but others find reminiscent of the countryside.

The roots of *Geranium maculatum*, wild crane's bill, were once used as a remedy for sore throats, ulcers, dysentery, and bleeding.

Phlox Family

With the exception of one species, the *Phlox* genus is native to North America.

Wild blue phlox, *Phlox divaricata*, native to eastern Canada and the United States, was one of the first New World plants taken back to Europe by early explorers. It is sometimes called wild sweet William.

Many cultivars of annual phlox have been created from *Phlox drummondii*, which once grew wild across south central Texas.

Iris Family

Preceding pages: Phlox subulata is commonly known as moss pink or mountain pink. It grows in a mat of thick mosslike leaves that are almost completely hidden in spring by the cheery flowers.

Irises are often called flags because of the way they flutter in the wind. Southern blue flag, *Iris virginica,* is native to wet coastal plains from Virginia to Texas.

One of the first signs of spring is the tiny crested iris, *Iris cristata.* Native Americans once used it in various medical treatments, but its use is no longer recommended.

The Douglas iris, *Iris douglasiana,* is native to the Pacific coast of the United States and, like all irises, has three upright petals called standards and three drooping petals called falls.

The iris was named for the
Greek goddess of the rainbow,
whose role often was to bring
peace after a confrontation.
Blooming in a true rainbow
of colors, the iris is the state
flower of Tennessee.

Yellow iris, *Iris pseudacorus,* is native
to Europe and North Africa, but is now
naturalized in wet areas across the United
States.

Madder Family

Plants in the *Hedyotis* genus were once classified as *Houstonia.* They were one of the colonists' favorite plants and remain popular today. Right: *Hedyotis caerulea* is commonly called bluet, for its dainty blue flowers.

Although *Linum* flowers are
rarely yellow, *Linum rigidum*
is one exception to the rule.
Native to the western United
States and Canada, it was
used by Native Americans for
a number of purposes, in-
cluding food and fabric.

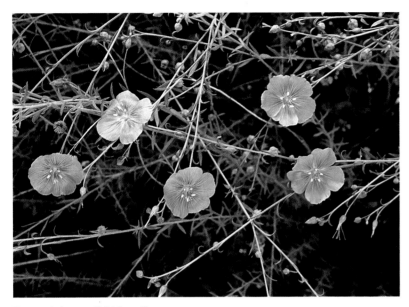

Perennial, or wild blue, flax,
Linum perenne, is native to
Europe but was brought to
North America by the early
settlers.

The fibrous stems of flax have, throughout the
ages, been used to make rope and cloth, and
its seeds have been eaten or pressed into oil.
The genus name, *Linum*, has lent its name to
lingerie, line, linen, and lint.

Water lilies, such as the blue waterlily, *Nymphaea elegans*, have large waxy leaves that float on the surface of the water, beautiful flowers, and a massive rootstock that creeps into the mud many feet below the water's surface.

The flowers of the American lotus, *Nelumbo lutea,* are huge. Often considered a sacred plant, the lotus has seeds that can remain viable for centuries.

Blooms of the white water lily, *Nymphaea odorata,* are open only from early morning until midday. The genus is named for the mythological nymphs of ancient Greece who lived in ponds and lakes.

When the flower of the water lily fades, the seed case becomes submerged until the seeds ripen and it splits open. The seeds float on the water until they become waterlogged, sink to the bottom, germinate, and grow.

Index of Photography

TIB indicates The Image Bank.

All photographs courtesy of PHOTO/NATS, except where indicated *.